SOCIETY FOR
HUMAN
RESOURCE
MANAGEMENT

AGE DISCRIMINATION IN THE WORKPLACE:

A PRIMER FOR HUMAN RESOURCE PROFESSIONALS

MCAFEE & TAFT
A Professional Corporation
Tenth Floor, Two Leadership Square
Oklahoma City, OK 73012

SHRM FOUNDATION
SOCIETY FOR HUMAN RESOURCE MANAGEMENT

This book is published by the Society for Human Resource Management (SHRM) and funded by a generous grant from the SHRM Foundation. As the R&D arm of the profession, the SHRM Foundation expands the body of human resource knowledge through its support of leading-edge research, practical publications, and educational initiatives. The interpretations, conclusions, and recommendations, however, are those of the authors and do not necessarily represent those of the Foundation or of SHRM.

The Society for Human Resource Management (SHRM) is the leading voice of the human resource profession. SHRM provides education and information services, conferences and seminars, government and media representation, online services, and publications to more than 110,000 professional and student members throughout the world. The Society, the world's largest human resource management association, is a founding member of the North American Human Resource Management Association (NAHRMA) and a founding member of the World Federation of Personnel Management Associations (WFPMA). On behalf of NAHRMA, SHRM also serves as President of WFPMA.

© 1999 Society for Human Resource Management

ISBN 0-939900-90-4

ACKNOWLEDGMENT

This book was authored by the labor, employment, and employee benefits practice group of McAfee & Taft, P.C., in Oklahoma City, Oklahoma. Contributing authors were Samuel R. Fulkerson, Michael F. Lauderdale, Gary C. Pierson, Tony G. Puckett, Kathy Reilly Teel, Peter T. Van Dyke, and Nathan L. Whatley. Special gratitude is expressed to Sam Fulkerson, who served as the managing editor.

McAfee & Taft's labor, employment, and employee benefits practice group conducts a national practice in all areas of employer/employee relations.

INTRODUCTION

We have written this book for the human resource professional and designed it to provide practical, day-to-day insight into common age discrimination issues. It may be read as a whole or by selected chapters, depending on the human resource manager's needs.

The book includes a chapter by Dr. Ross P. Laguzza of DecisionQuest, Inc. DecisionQuest, among many other capabilities, assists trial lawyers in understanding how jurors make decisions. DecisionQuest's insight into the psychology of juries in employment cases is fascinating and, obviously, enormously helpful. We have always felt it important for human resource managers to understand how jurors will judge managers' employment decisions so that decisions can be made prudently. The participation of Dr. Laguzza and DecisionQuest is, as always, greatly appreciated.

TABLE OF CONTENTS

CHAPTER 1

WHAT IS AGE DISCRIMINATION?

To discriminate is to recognize or perceive differences between things. The act of discrimination also includes showing preference for something, usually to the exclusion of something else. Therefore, a person discriminates when he or she chooses between things. There is nothing unlawful about the act of discriminating, generally speaking, and we all do it on a daily basis in making decisions, whether of a personal nature or business related.

To be sure, the word "discrimination" has fallen into the pejorative with the rise of the civil rights movement over the course of the last generation. Now, rather than indicating a well-founded distinction, the word is commonly understood to mean the act of showing prejudice, that is, an unfounded and unfavorable attitude, toward minority groups in our society.

AGE DISCRIMINATION IN EMPLOYMENT

The civil rights movement also has resulted in a series of laws making it unlawful for employers to discriminate against persons in their employment on the basis of certain personal characteristics. Among those characteristics now protected is age.

The characteristic of age, however, is different from other legally protected characteristics, such as race and gender. When Congress enacted the Civil Rights Act of 1964, making race, color, national origin, religion, and sex into protected classes, it deliberately omitted age, that is, "older persons," as a protected class. Instead, Congress directed the Secretary of Labor to investigate age discrimination in employment to determine whether it was of a magnitude to warrant congressional action and, if so, to make recommendations for addressing it.

The result was a report confirming that age bias exists in the workplace, especially in the context of hiring and termination decisions.

The report, however, also concluded that age discrimination is different from other types of employment discrimination in at least three important respects. First, unlike racial bias, no history of overt bias exists against older persons as a class. The explanation lies, in large part, in the second distinction: a person's age changes over time, unlike immutable characteristics such as race and gender, and all persons will join the class of "older persons" if they live long enough. The fact that the protected trait is universal in this sense lessens the degree of bias against the protected class. Finally, in certain circumstances there actually may be a correlation between age and ability to perform certain types of jobs, which, again, is unlike a characteristic such as race.

As the report explained:

> [The Secretary of Labor finds] no significant evidence of ... the kind of dislike or intolerance that sometimes exists in the case of race, color, religion, or national origin, and which is based on considerations entirely unrelated to ability to perform a job.

> We do find substantial evidence of ... discrimination based on unsupported general assumptions about the effect of age on ability [to perform a job].

> We find that ... [in the context of] decisions made about aging and the ability to perform in individual cases, there may or may not be arbitrary discrimination on the basis of age, depending on the individual circumstances.

The report further explained the difference between age discrimination and other types of employment discrimination as follows:

> Discrimination in employment based on race, religion, color, or national origin is accompanied by and often has its origins in prejudices that originate *outside the sphere of employment*. There are no such prejudices in American life which apply to older persons and which would carry strongly into the sphere of employment.

> The process of aging is inescapable, affecting everyone who lives long enough. It is gradual, minimizing and obscuring differences among people. At all times there are people of all ages living in close association rather than in separate and distinct social or economic environments. The element of intolerance, of such overriding importance in the case of attitudes toward other groups, assumes

minimal importance in the case of older people and older workers.

It is true that hiring officials are not immune to the brightness, vigor, and the attraction of youth, and they are not always above exploiting these attributes for commercial advantage. But those choices involve preferences for one group, rather than antagonism against another.

The issue of discrimination revolves around the nature of the work and its rewards, in relation to the ability or presumed ability of people at various ages, rather than around the people as such. The issue thus differs greatly from the primary one involved in discrimination on the basis of race, color, religion, or national origin, which is basically unrelated to ability to perform work.

The Secretary of Labor concluded that older persons are at a disadvantage in relation to younger persons in the modern economy, especially when they are displaced at a relatively advanced age and must compete for new employment. The Secretary recommended passage of a federal law promoting employment of persons on the basis of ability rather than age, prohibiting arbitrary age discrimination in employment, and helping employers and employees find ways of meeting problems arising from the ways that age affects employment.

THE AGE DISCRIMINATION IN EMPLOYMENT ACT

Congress responded in 1967 by passing the Age Discrimination in Employment Act (ADEA), which prohibits discrimination, that is, the making of unfounded and unfavorable decisions, in employment-related matters on the basis of a person's age.

The ADEA makes it unlawful for any employer with 20 or more employees to take any of the following actions against persons age 40 or older:

To fail or refuse to hire or to discharge any individual or otherwise discriminate against any individual with respect to his compensation, terms, conditions, or privileges of employment, because of such individual's age; [or]

To limit, segregate, or classify ... employees in any way which would deprive or tend to deprive any individual of employment opportunities or otherwise adversely affect his status as an employee, because of such individual's age ...

The ADEA covers almost every aspect of the employment relationship, and it prohibits age discrimination not only by private employers of the requisite size, but also by employment agencies, labor unions, and the federal and state governments.

The ADEA, in summary, makes it unlawful for employers to make decisions adversely affecting persons age 40 or older simply because of their age or because of stereotypes associated with age; for example, some stereotypes are that productivity necessarily declines with age, that older employees are not adaptable to change, or that older employees will not be around as long as younger employees. It should be self-evident that none of these stereotypes is accurate and certainly not to a sufficient degree to serve as the basis for an adverse employment decision. Instead, an employment decision based on such stereotypes is arbitrary.

At the heart of the ADEA is the elimination of stereotypical thinking about the effects of age on the ability to work. For example, stereotypical perceptions about declining ability to perform may result in a negative, and incorrect, assessment of an older person's abilities. The problem is compounded by the fact that in some instances an objective basis may exist for concluding that age and diminished performance capacity have a correlation. For example, physical limitations such as diminishment in strength and aerobic capacity generally become greater as age increases. If those types of physical capacities are essential to effective job performance, then there may be a correlation between age and ability to perform satisfactorily.

The ADEA, however, prohibits stereotyping and requires employers to recognize that older persons, for example, may compensate for any diminution in physical capacity with superior experience, maturity, and problem-solving skills. In other words, the message of the ADEA is that as we age we may perform work differently, but overall ability and quality generally remain at least comparable. Therefore, even assuming the existence of some correlation between age and performance, employers, in making employment-related decisions, are required by federal law to make an individualized, case-by-case assessment of a person's ability to perform.

Nonetheless, the ADEA reflects that age as a legally protected characteristic is different from other protected characteristics, for the reasons discussed above. As a result, the ADEA limits employer liability in certain circumstances, recognizes different defenses to age discrimination claims, and provides for different and lesser kinds of damages for violations, as discussed in following chapters.

The ADEA also does not require employers to give preferential treatment to protected-age persons. For example, the law does not require employers to maintain or increase the numbers of older persons in its workforce. Employers are allowed to exercise business judgment in running their operations, as long as the reasons relied on are not a pretext or cover-up for age discrimination.

THE AGING LABOR FORCE

The ADEA will assume even greater prominence for employers in the near future because of America's aging labor force. In 1994, approximately 131 million persons worked in the private sector labor force. Of those, approximately 40 million were age 45 or older. By 2005, the total labor force is expected to grow to approximately 147 million persons, of which approximately 57 million will be age 45 or older. So, for the period 1994–2005 the segment of the private sector labor force age 45 and older is expected to grow by more than 40 percent. Furthermore, of the approximately 57 million persons age 45 and older in the private sector labor force in 2005, it is projected that more than 22 million of them will be age 55 and older, a significant increase in the size of that labor force segment over 1994.

This change in labor force demographics obviously is a result of the aging of the "baby boom" generation, that is, persons born between 1946 and 1964. By 2005, the last of the baby boomers will move into the protected age group. Sheer numbers alone should make it plain that employers must actively review employment policies and practices to ensure that age bias is not a factor in any decision-making process. The increase in protected-age participants in the labor force also will require improvement in management training on age-related issues. With the aging of the private sector labor force in the near future, those employers who ignore, tolerate, or engage in age-based decision-making will be exposed to significantly greater risk of age discrimination litigation.

THE TYPICAL AGE DISCRIMINATION PLAINTIFF

Additional factors should be considered in gauging the effects of an aging labor force. First, although the labor force is aging, the average age of age discrimination plaintiffs apparently is declining. Whereas the typical age discrimination plaintiff once was a male in his mid 50s, recent data indicate a significant increase in age discrimination plaintiffs in the 40–49 age grouping. Recent data also indicate a notable increase in female age discrimination plaintiffs over the last 10 years. If the data accurately reflect a trend toward the feminization and relative youth of claimants, it can be concluded that the pool of potential age discrimination plaintiffs will grow rapidly in the next few years.

Another factor compounding the effect of the aging labor force is self-inflicted by employers; it is the increasing use of mass reductions in force as a management tool. At least one reputable study has found that the layoff rate more than doubled between 1980 and 1992. Nor are there any signs that the trend is abating. It should be obvious that if reductions in force have become routine management practice, then the aging of the labor force will result in more mass displacements of protected-age persons, thus increasing the risk of age-related litigation.

Finally, although this observation is a subjective one, the baby boomer generation is relatively well educated as a group, and it has matured in an age of civil rights development and entitlement mentality. The combination of these factors and those cited above makes the growth of protected-age labor force participants an ominous trend for employers engaging in actual age discrimination or, what is more likely, those employers who simply are perceived by employees as tolerating age bias.

CHAPTER 2

CLAIMS AND DEFENSES

Employers may be sued for age discrimination under two basic theories of liability: *disparate treatment theory* and *disparate impact theory*.

DISPARATE TREATMENT CLAIMS

Disparate treatment occurs when an employer intentionally discriminates against an employee, or prospective employee, because of his or her age. In a disparate treatment claim, the focus is on the individual employee, who ultimately must prove that the employer *intentionally* discriminated against him because of his age.

Evidence of intentional age discrimination is almost always "circumstantial" rather than "direct." In other words, an employee usually proves intentional age bias by showing factual circumstances that allow reasonable persons to conclude that age was a motivating factor in the challenged employment decision, although the employer steadfastly denies the allegation. An employee rarely is able to show direct evidence of unlawful age bias by producing, for example, a company memo stating that the employer was making a conscious effort to reduce the age of its workforce at the time of the challenged termination.

The typical disparate treatment claim involves a terminated employee who brings suit alleging that younger, less qualified employees were retained in the same position he or she once held. Often, the claimant also will allege that management members or the actual decision-maker made age-related remarks close in time to his or her termination; for example, "We need young blood in this company," or "We need to get rid of the deadwood." If the terminated employee can show this type of circumstantial evidence, and the employer does not effectively refute it, the law allows a judge or jury to conclude that the difference in treatment between the older and younger employees is attributable to age bias.

DISPARATE IMPACT CLAIMS

The second basic theory of liability is called disparate impact theory. Under this theory, the employee is not required to show intentional age discrimination. Rather, disparate impact liability occurs when some employment practice or policy, neutral as to age on its face, tends to have a disproportionate, adverse effect on protected-age employees. In short, a disparate impact claim involves an employment practice that is fair in form but discriminatory in operation. This type of claim commonly involves statistical and demographic analyses of the relevant workforce, which is discussed at length in chapter 5.

For example, if an employer relied on salary level as a selection criterion in a reduction in force by terminating all employees at or above a certain salary level, then the action could result in the termination of a disproportionate number of protected-age employees because salary levels tend to increase over time. Because increased age has a general correlation with salary, the employer could be liable for age discrimination under a disparate impact theory, even though it did not consciously intend to discriminate against older persons.

It must be noted that many courts refuse to apply disparate impact theory to age discrimination claims, and the trend is in that direction. This fact is significant because the type of claim that may be brought against an employer is then limited to an intentional discrimination claim. The United States Supreme Court, however, has not decided the question, although it has indicated that the theory does not apply to age discrimination claims. Employers must determine through legal counsel whether they are subject to the jurisdiction of a court that recognizes disparate impact theory under the ADEA.

Prudent employers, regardless, will scrutinize employment policies and practices to determine the existence of a potential adverse impact on protected-age employees. Even in those places where an employer may not be subject to disparate impact liability, an employee alleging intentional age discrimination may be allowed to use evidence of a neutral employment practice that has an adverse impact on older employees as circumstantial evidence of *intentional* age discrimination.

OTHER THEORIES OF LIABILITY

Most types of employment discrimination claims may be asserted under the ADEA, including, for example, constructive discharge, retaliation, "pattern and practice," and class action and harassment claims.

Retaliation claims typically arise when a current employee files a charge with the Equal Employment Opportunity Commission (EEOC), or a state human rights agency, alleging age discrimination for, by way of example, denial of a promotion. If the employee subsequently is demoted or terminated, he or she may bring a claim of retaliation under the ADEA for the earlier age discrimination charge.

An employee need not be in the protected age group to bring a retaliation claim under the ADEA. An employee under age 40 may have a claim if he can show he was retaliated against for participating in age-related activity by providing, for example, a supporting statement for a protected-age co-worker alleging age discrimination.

"Pattern and practice" claims involve allegations that intentional age discrimination is an employer's common operating procedure. In these claims, a former employee will allege that he or she is simply one of many employees who has fallen victim to the intentionally discriminatory employment practice. The claim, however, is brought by an individual employee or a small group of employees and is different from a class action.

Class actions, also called "collective actions" under the ADEA, are becoming commonplace. Class actions, depending on where the action is filed, may be based on either disparate treatment or disparate impact–type allegations.

A newly developing theory of liability is called "age harassment." This theory of liability is an outgrowth of sexual harassment law. Age harassment liability may exist where age-related conduct or comments are sufficiently severe or pervasive to create a hostile working environment for the protected-age employee. Examples of conduct that could result in a hostile working environment include repeated age-related remarks, even supposedly humorous remarks, and tangible mistreatment such as disparity in wages and assignment to less favorable job tasks. In this instance, a protected-age employee may have a claim for age harassment even though he remains employed. Alternatively, an employee may link an age harassment claim with a constructive discharge claim.

DEFENSES TO DISPARATE TREATMENT CLAIMS

Employers use a variety of defenses to age discrimination claims. Most defenses apply to disparate treatment claims. There are distinct defenses to disparate impact claims, which are addressed separately.

Attacking the Prima Facie Case

The first defense to an intentional discrimination claim is to demonstrate that the employee cannot make the required initial showing, called the *prima facie* case. For an age claim, an employee must show at the outset that he is a member of the protected age group (age 40 or older), that he was qualified for the job at issue and was adequately performing his job duties, that he experienced an adverse employment decision, and that younger employees were treated more favorably, that is, were hired or retained in his stead. This final bit of evidence is necessary to support a reasonable inference that the challenged decision was motivated by unlawful age bias.

An employer may successfully defend a claim by showing that the employee's proof fails at one step of the *prima facie* case. Most commonly, the employer shows that the employee was not adequately performing his job duties at the time of the challenged employment decision or that any younger persons hired or retained were better qualified individuals. An employee's initial showing also may be challenged by demonstrating that the persons treated more favorably were only marginally younger than the employee. For example, if the person hired or retained is only four to five years younger than the employee, a court may find the age difference too insignificant to support a reasonable presumption that the employer's decision was motivated by age bias.

Legitimate, Nondiscriminatory Reason

The ADEA states that an employer may discipline or discharge an employee for "good cause." This language serves as the basis for the most common defense to an intentional age discrimination claim, which is simply to assert that the challenged employment decision was the result of a "legitimate, nondiscriminatory reason." A nondiscriminatory reason may include any reason other than age; it does not have to be a business-related reason, nor does it have to support a "just cause" termination. Employers with unionized workforces are cautioned that "just cause" in the context of a collective bargaining agreement is different from the ADEA's "good cause" concept.

Even an irrational or incorrect reason for a challenged employment decision is lawful under the ADEA, as long as it is not a pretext or cover-up for age bias. An employer may be completely mistaken about the accuracy of the reason for a termination, but that mistake generally does not make its actions unlawful. For example, an employer may base a termination decision on an incorrect belief that an employee willfully violated company policy, when in fact he did not. In the event of an age discrimination claim, the employer need only produce evidence that the challenged decision resulted from the employer's sincere but mistaken belief about the employee's misconduct; the employer is not required to prove actual misconduct and should not be liable simply for being wrong.

A few courts, however, require that an employer not only have a genuine belief in the asserted reason, but also have a reasonable belief that the reason is accurate. In other words, these courts place a duty on the employer to determine the accuracy of an asserted reason before actually relying on it. The thinking behind this approach is that adversely affecting the employment relationship is sufficiently serious to warrant requiring employers to make adequately informed decisions.

When it comes to the nondiscriminatory reason defense, the rule of thumb is that the more unlikely or erroneous the reason given for the challenged decision, the less likely it will be persuasive to a judge or jury.

Typical nondiscriminatory reasons include excessive absenteeism, failing to comply with a call-in policy while on sick or medical leave, and, most commonly, unsatisfactory job performance. In a reduction-in-force scenario, typical reasons include relatively poor performance in comparison with persons in the same or similar job title, and job elimination. In the hiring scenario, typical reasons include that the applicant was not among the best-qualified candidates.

With a disparate treatment claim, the key issue usually is the decision-maker's state of mind at the time of the challenged decision. As a result, the asserted nondiscriminatory reason must actually have caused the challenged decision. An employer may not rely on a reason not discovered until after the decision was made. Obviously, a reason not known at the time of the decision could not have motivated it.

An employer who relies on the nondiscriminatory-reason defense only has to produce some evidence of the asserted reason's validity. The employer does not have the burden to actually prove, that is, convince the judge or jury, that the asserted reason caused the challenged decision—at least in theory. For example, an employer only has to produce an affidavit or a knowledgeable witness stating that the asserted reason was in fact the basis for the challenged decision. An employer is not required to justify that decision, to explain discrepancies in facts, or to address alternative explanations for the decision. Practically speaking, however, every employer ending up as a defendant in an age discrimination claim carries the burden of proof on each material issue. As discussed in other chapters, employers rarely get a jury of their peers, and juries generally demand that employers prove their case conclusively before finding in their favor.

Once an employer has produced evidence supporting its asserted nondiscriminatory reason, the employee must prove that the asserted reason is not true but, instead, that it is a pretext or cover-up for age discrimination.

IF AGE WAS A FACTOR

A number of defenses exist for which an employer carries the burden of proof both in theory and actuality. These defenses are used when age is an acknowledged or proven factor in the challenged decision. The defenses are the bona fide occupational qualification (BFOQ), bona fide seniority system, bona fide benefit plan, and "mixed motives" defenses.

Bona Fide Occupational Qualification

A BFOQ defense typically involves a situation in which an employer acknowledges that the challenged employment decision was based on age. The ADEA allows employers under certain circumstances to make age-based decisions when age is a bona fide occupational qualification reasonably necessary to the employer's business operation. The BFOQ defense is often asserted when public safety is at issue, such as when an airline has implemented a mandatory retirement age for pilots.

In order to establish a BFOQ defense an employer must make a two-part showing: (1) it first must show that age as a qualification is reasonably necessary to the employer's core business operations; and (2) it must show either that there is a rational basis for believing that most or all members of the protected age group cannot safely perform the job duties at issue, or that it would be impractical to make an individualized determination of the affected class members' abilities.

The first element requires employers to demonstrate that persons above a certain age generally are not qualified to perform a job that is essential to their operations. The second element may be demonstrated by use of physical examinations or, alternatively, an employer may demonstrate that individualized testing of affected persons is impractical because, for example, such testing would not reveal whether individual group members are prone to age-related conditions that present a threat to safety. If employers establish both elements, they may be able to lawfully require mandatory retirement at a certain age or to refuse to hire persons above a certain age.

The BFOQ defense is applicable only in very narrow circumstances, and courts construe it strictly.

Bona Fide Seniority System

A seniority system gives preferential treatment to employees on the basis of length of service; that is, the longer they have been employed, the greater their employment rights or entitlements. Formal seniority systems or plans are most often found in unionized workplaces, where the systems are of central importance and are the subject of negotiation between labor and management. However, seniority systems also exist in non-union settings, where an employer may unilaterally implement a system in certain circumstances.

The bona fide seniority system defense allows employers to base decisions on employee seniority accrued under a legitimate seniority system. For example, an employer may lawfully refuse to hire a protected-age job applicant because a younger applicant has greater prior seniority under a legitimate plan. The seniority system, however, cannot be a subterfuge for age discrimination.

Bona Fide Benefit Plan

The ADEA is intended to protect against discrimination in employee benefits, but it provides a defense when an age-based disparity in benefits results from the effect of a bona fide benefit plan. The defense, or exception, essentially allows lesser benefits for older employees as long as it is the result of age-related cost considerations. For example, if it costs more to provide a benefit such as health insurance to older employees than it does to provide the same benefit to younger employees, an employer may provide reduced benefits to older employees as long as the employer spends the same amount of money overall for older and younger employees.

The bona fide benefit plan exception simply recognizes a possible differential in benefit costs because of age factors that are beyond the employer's control. It allows an adjustment in benefit levels if the employer spends the same amount of money on both younger and older employees. This exception is sometimes described as the "equal benefit or equal cost" rule.

Mixed Motives

The ADEA also recognizes a "mixed motives" defense in those situations in which both lawful factors and age bias caused the challenged decision. This defense usually is raised when an employee produces "direct evidence" of age discrimination. For example, an employee may produce evidence that the decision-maker stated to a third party that the challenged decision was motivated by age bias. In that event, an employer still may prevail by showing that the challenged decision would have been made anyway for lawful reasons, that is, even if the decision-maker had not been motivated at least in part by unlawful age bias.

Notably, the mixed motives defense is applied differently in age discrimination claims than in other types of employment discrimination claims. Previously, a successful mixed motives showing was a complete defense to liability in all types of employment discrimination claims. Congress, however, amended federal law (the Civil Rights Act of 1991) so that in all but age discrimination claims the mixed motives defense serves only to limit the type and amount of potential damages. Therefore, in all types of employment discrimination claims, save for age discrimination, even if an employer establishes a mixed motives defense it still will be liable for unlawful discrimination, but the amount of a plaintiff's recovery will be significantly limited.

DEFENSES TO DISPARATE IMPACT CLAIMS

Assuming that a disparate impact claim may be asserted under the ADEA, employers have a handful of defenses, although fewer than are available to disparate treatment claims. The first defense is simply to show that the challenged employment practice does not actually result in an adverse impact on protected-age employees. This defense often is accomplished by showing that an employee's supposed "statistical analysis" is invalid, as is discussed in chapter 5.

The second defense is to show that the challenged practice is job related and consistent with business necessity. The job-related aspect requires the employer to show that the challenged employment practice is somehow related to predicting or improving job performance. For example, if the challenged practice is a testing procedure used in the hiring process, then the employer may be required to show that the test measures skills or attributes necessary to satisfactory job performance.

The business necessity element requires an employer to demonstrate a business purpose behind the challenged employment practice, which is usually done by showing that the practice is necessary to an efficient or safe business operation. In short, an employer must be able to show that the challenged employment practice tends to measure or improve job performance in a particular job and efficiency in the business operation itself.

An employee or applicant may successfully challenge that showing by demonstrating that available alternative practices exist that would result in the same level of efficiency but without adversely affecting the protected age group.

MANDATORY RETIREMENT

The ADEA prohibits employers from forcing retirement-eligible employees into retirement and from imposing mandatory retirement ages, with limited exceptions. A mandatory retirement age may be permissible if it is a bona fide occupational qualification. For example, an employer may be able to justify a mandatory retirement age on the basis of safety considerations, such as the airline pilot scenario discussed above.

A forced retirement of a retirement-eligible employee may come within the "reasonable factors other than age" exception if the retirement is essentially in lieu of termination for good cause.

The ADEA also provides an exception for "bona fide executives or high policymakers." Under this exception, compulsory retirement of any employee who has reached age 65 and who is employed in a bona fide executive or high policy-making position may be justified. This exception also requires the employee's immediate entitlement to a minimum amount of retirement benefits. Compulsory retirement also may be lawful under certain circumstances for some employees of institutions of higher education, certain federal employees, and certain municipal employees, such as police officers and firefighters.

Employers may not mischaracterize an involuntary retirement program as a voluntary incentive program to avoid ADEA prohibitions. For example, although the ADEA's ban on mandatory retirement ages does not keep employers from using voluntary incentive or retirement programs to reduce workforce numbers, an employee's decision to participate in such a program must be truly voluntary. For example, if employees of a certain age are offered early retirement, but they face termination if they do not take advantage of the program, then the program is, in effect, the imposition of a mandatory retirement age, which violates the ADEA.

However, if an employer is carrying out a reduction in force, selects employees for termination, and then allows them to opt for involuntary early retirement if they are a certain age, then the actions are allowable. In that instance, the employees already have been selected for termination on the basis of other factors, and the offer of the early retirement option does not affect that determination.

STATE LAWS AGAINST AGE DISCRIMINATION

This chapter addresses federal law, but virtually every state has some type of antidiscrimination or fair employment practices statute prohibiting age discrimination in employment. Obviously, a review of state laws is beyond the scope of this book, but one basic point should be understood about the interplay between the ADEA and state laws. The ADEA is intended to work in concert with state antidiscrimination laws; it does not preempt or displace them.

As a result, in states with a law prohibiting age discrimination an employee may simultaneously assert claims under both state and federal law. If the state law provides an employee with greater protections or more generous remedies, the ADEA does not limit the scope of the state law. For example, it is generally agreed that under the ADEA a prevailing employee may not recover damages for emotional distress or punitive damages. Under some state laws, in contrast, employees may recover those types of damages and the ADEA cannot be relied on to curtail the state law recovery. (Damages issues are discussed in chapter 11.) Instead, the ADEA simply serves as a "floor," or minimum level of protection against age discrimination. The states are free to provide different and greater protections.

CHAPTER 3

REDUCTIONS IN FORCE

Employers have many reasons to conduct reductions in force (RIFs). The reasons include cost-cutting measures, replacement of human capital with technology, discontinuing antiquated business practices, streamlining operations, and moving production overseas. Regardless of the business justification for a reduction in force, the goal and results are always the same—employees are involuntarily separated from employment.

The increased use of reductions in force in the 1980s, as noted in chapter 1, fostered remarkable resentment as breadwinners and parents in large numbers were forced into unemployment. Even the associated terminology became offensive to many, as both companies and their employees were "right-sized." It did not take long for employee representatives to publicly criticize the effects of "right-sizing" not only on laid-off employees but also on their families.

The reductions in force of the 1980s and the arguably insensitive nomenclature used with them generated a great deal of age discrimination litigation, which has continued into the present. The reduction-in-force age discrimination case is difficult to defend principally because the employee has shown no inappropriate behavior. That fact, combined with the relatively advanced age and long seniority of many laid-off employees, creates a powerful mixture both from a legal and an emotional standpoint. Compounding the situation is the fact that juries typically consist not of employers, but of employees who have been laid off themselves, who are related to someone who has been laid off, or who know someone who has joined the ranks of the unemployed via a reduction in force. (Jury-related issues are discussed in chapter 9.)

The most difficult of all reduction-in-force cases, from the employer's perspective, is the long-term employee who has reached or passed age 50, who has had satisfactory, if not stellar, job evaluations, and who has been selected in a reduction in force designed to increase shareholder value. The emotional turmoil created by this type of scenario is difficult not only on the litigants but also on the jurors. After all, the typical juror is or has been an employee and is either within the protected class or fully expects to become a member.

With this situation in mind, certain reduction-in-force characteristics are not only defensible, but also can be palatable to those adversely affected. Those characteristics are outlined in this chapter. It should always be remembered, however, that if a reduction in force is challenged legally, the final arbiter of how successfully it was planned and implemented will be either a judge or jury. Consequently, the observations in this chapter are based not only on a review of many different corporate approaches to reductions in force and subsequent attempts to explain them to juries, but also on insights provided by cooperative jurors after reduction-in-force trials.

ARTICULATED BUSINESS REASON

Corporations do not lay off workers simply because they can—they always have a business reason. Many times, however, the employer either will not or cannot clearly articulate why a reduction in force was implemented. It is tempting—but inaccurate—to state that an employer must articulate why a reduction in force is "necessary." In other words, reductions in force do not have to be the choice of last resort. They may be strategic business decisions that are based on what is best for the organization, even if the company is doing quite well.

The first step to conducting a successful reduction in force is to have a sound and easy-to-explain business reason for it. Clever words and phrases do not suffice. If an employer is sending jobs overseas, for example, the company should say so directly and be prepared to show why it chose to do so. It should not call its decision an "effort to improve market share by hiring a multinational workforce," as that type of corporate doublespeak is obvious to everyone. The more straightforward and business related the reason is for a reduction in force, the easier it is to defend it against age discrimination claims.

Plenty of legal cases say an employee does not have the right to second-guess the business judgment of the employer and, therefore, the former employee cannot challenge the soundness of the employer's business decisions. However, *every* age discrimination case ever reported also states that the laid-off employee can challenge the truthfulness of the employer's asserted reasons and, by showing those reasons are not true or are otherwise pretextual, can raise an inference of illegal discrimination.

For example, a well-known case involved an employer's claim that the challenged reduction in force was caused by poor economic conditions. On its face, the asserted reason was plausible. However, and unfortunately for the employer, the company's annual report published three months after the reduction in force showed record profits. The asserted reason for the reduction in force obviously was inconsistent with the facts, thus bringing into question whether the reduction actually was a ruse to reduce the age of the company workforce. Even worse, the former employee also was able to show that she had been replaced by a younger person shortly after her termination. Not surprisingly, the employer lost the age discrimination case that ensued, and lost big. Many employers will read this example and think to themselves that they would never do anything so unsound, but the law books are full of similar cases and verdicts.

Another benefit of a well-defined business reason has nothing to do with legal requirements but, rather, is derived strictly from the psychological effect that reductions in force have on affected employees and the juries that may ultimately judge their legality. If challenged in court, and despite instructions to the contrary, juries are going to ask themselves whether the actions of the company were "fair" and make their decision on that basis.

Our understanding of the psychological outlook of the average juror toward reductions in force is important if we are to better understand how and why reduction-in-force processes should be designed and implemented. Jurors should be recognized for who they are—people with both good and bad employment experiences and with families and friends who have been terminated or laid off. Acting in the role of jurors, they are perhaps experiencing their first taste of power and control over an employer. It can be pretty heady stuff. They will not dispassionately review a company's decisions, studying events in isolation; instead, they will look at the big picture. If they cannot become comfortable with the reason for the reduction in force, then the actual employee selection process used by the employer will become meaningless in their deliberation. Two reasons particularly difficult for jurors to accept are reductions in force resulting from an already-successful company's desire to make more money and reductions in which so-called "American jobs" are shipped overseas to take advantage of lower labor costs.

Whatever the corporate reason for a reduction in force, however, it must be communicated clearly and succinctly. Anything short of that communication will often negate otherwise good procedures used in the reduction's implementation.

ORGANIZATION

Behavioral scientists tell us that if a corporation is going to affect people's lives in a dramatic way, it better have not only a good reason for doing so but also a well-conceived plan. This precaution is called for because the average person believes that while it may be okay for individuals to be disorganized in their personal or professional lives, the first order of business for all corporations is to operate efficiently and rationally. As we will see in chapter 9, Dr. Ross P. Laguzza and his colleagues at DecisionQuest say that corporations which are perceived as handling significant events such as reductions in force in a disorganized manner are considered "unsafe," that is, out of control and adversely affecting peoples' lives in a haphazard way. Obviously, no one wants to be treated arbitrarily, and jurors are quite willing to send a message, via an unfavorable verdict, to a disorganized employer in the hope that their current employers pay heed.

Companies can do a number of things, as discussed below, to avoid being perceived as "unsafe" employers.

Neutral Administrators

A good first step in developing a defensible reduction-in-force program is to create a team of "neutral" administrators who will design, carry out, and ensure fairness throughout the reduction-in-force process. The oversight team should be neutral in the sense that its members are not involved in making individual termination decisions unless those decisions are based on strictly objective criteria, such as seniority. Such a team should be composed of employees of different races, genders, and ages, not only to give an appearance of diversity, but also to actually ensure diverse input.

The need for neutrality in the oversight team should be self-evident. You must remember that many employees sincerely believe that their managers are biased one way or another toward all subordinate employees. When those managers are involved not only in selection decisions but also in the development of the selection system, suspicion and criticism will run rampant. In other words, a company that allows the same people who design a selection system to also make selection decisions effectively destroys the opportunity to foster a sense of fairness and objectivity about the system in the at-risk workforce. One should never forget that, in an area such as this one, perception is reality.

Another critical element to an effective oversight team is a strong commitment to confidentiality. Ideas about the reduction-in-force process, whether good or bad, must not be discussed with or circulated among employees. Allowing that to happen results in an atmosphere of distrust among team members, which hinders the free exchange of ideas and spawns unproductive workplace gossip. The requirement of confidentiality should be repeated every time the oversight team meets.

As one might suspect, the human resources department is usually the best place to begin when putting together an oversight team.

However, nothing suggests that an oversight team should be composed only of human resource employees. Again, depending on the size of the employer and the reduction in force, an employer may find it advantageous to involve management employees from different areas, perhaps even from areas unaffected by the reduction. Also, some of the best oversight teams we have encountered, especially from the employees' perspective, have included a nonmanagement employee with significant seniority. Nonmanagement involvement should not only foster a perception of fairness, but also provide a different perspective about the reduction-in-force process and its potential effects.

The first task of an oversight team should be to review the reasons for the reduction in force with upper management and to help formulate the official corporate position on why the reduction is to be implemented. The oversight team can help put business reasons into easily understood language and often serves to "soften" a numbers-driven or poorly articulated reason. This type of interaction between the oversight team and upper management should continue throughout the reduction in force.

A note of caution about team dynamics is necessary. Oversight teams that become too big tend to be less useful. Sheer size can stymie exchange of ideas and effective decision-making, resulting in "decisions by committee" or, what is worse, managerial "vapor lock" where nothing can be decided. Depending on the size of the layoff, an effective oversight team of three to five persons can comfortably handle most related tasks.

In summary, the team approach is good because it allows for the exchange of ideas before making and implementing significant decisions; it provides a system of checks and balances, thus lessening the chances for ill-advised decisions; and it also begins the process of creating a sense of perceived fairness in the employees who are at risk in the reduction in force. The team concept is far superior to the "lone ranger" approach in which only the head of human resources plans the reduction in force and, in some cases, decides who is to be laid off.

Selection Criteria

Once management and the oversight team have framed the reasons for the reduction in force, the next order of business is to develop and state the criteria for layoff selections. In doing so, it is imperative that the oversight team first review all previously published employee communications, such as employee handbooks and policy statements, for statements on layoff criteria. If an employee publication states how reductions in force will take place, the employer is best advised to be consistent with prior statements or expect to suffer the allegation that any modification was a pretext for a new, discriminatory system. If selection criteria have not been addressed previously, at least not in writing, criteria should be developed *for the current reduction only.*

An employer may be satisfied with a reduction-in-force program, including selection criteria, and may anticipate using it again; however, employers should bear in mind that times, people, and the business climate change. Therefore, it is always wise to retain flexibility in planning areas. Flexibility in reduction-in-force matters can be preserved simply by publishing a statement to the effect that the current selection criteria and related matters were developed for the present reduction only. This communication will undermine legal challenges that otherwise could be based on changes in current selection criteria, such as a challenge to performance-based criteria because past reductions were seniority based.

The oversight team may settle on one or many selection criteria, and they may be subjective or objective in nature. The most common purely objective criterion is seniority. It is certainly the easiest criterion to administer and the most defensible, but it does not ensure that the best workforce is retained. As a result, it has become quite rare for reductions in force to be purely seniority based, happening most often in union or quasi-union settings. Instead, because the universal goal for employers is to retain the best employees during downsizings, a combination of subjective and objective criteria is typically used. Selection criteria usually include a combination of factors such as performance, attendance, flexibility (cross-training), potential, seniority, job requirements, future company needs, and the like. As a rule, however, the greater the number and the more abstract the criteria, the more important it is to reach consensus about working definitions before applying them.

It is often surprisingly difficult to define selection criteria. If the criteria are not easily defined, they should be reviewed again because their appropriateness is questionable. Employers will have a quite difficult time defending criteria that even the oversight team does not understand.

Even objective criteria can lead to confusion if their meaning and application are not properly defined. For example, most people think they know what "seniority" means in the employment context. However, in specific application, seniority may mean overall tenure at the company or it could mean seniority in a particular department or function.

The same is true with the objective concept of "performance." In its purest sense, performance is the sum of all other criteria. Certainly, such things as attendance, productivity, flexibility, and others add up to an employee's total performance quotient. However, most employers choose to subdivide these into separate criteria and include performance as a distinct measure of historical effort, and not a projection of future effort. This example illustrates that everyone—controlling management, the oversight team, and selecting managers—needs to be on the same page regarding definitions and application of criteria. Otherwise, inconsistency will arise, and inconsistency is extremely difficult to explain and defend in age discrimination claims.

Although objective criteria are rarely challenged in legal actions, subjective criteria almost always are. Accordingly, defining the scope and use of subjective criteria is especially important. For example, "potential" is a common reduction-in-force criterion. However, in more than one case in which the concept of "potential" was ill defined by an employer, it has been suggested that "potential is a code word for youth." Although such a conclusion is illogical upon examination, it has an initial surface appeal, and that may be as far as a jury looks. The conclusion is illogical because persons of any age can have—or lack—the potential to improve performance. Many 20-year-olds, by all appearances, have little or no potential, and an equal number of protected-age employees have no potential, either. At the same time, there are employees of all ages who have exceptional potential. In short, potential is not an age-related concept.

Not only is potential a subjective criterion, but the yardstick for measuring it is not constant; assessing the potential of a mailroom employee is different from evaluating that of the chief financial officer. As a rule, a direct relationship exists between the level and complexity of the position held and the subjectivity of measurements necessary to grade overall performance. For example, it is relatively easy to assess the performance of a machine operator who makes widgets all day. Grading the performance of the executive vice president of bionuclear development is somewhat more difficult, however.

That subject leads us to an important point—no rule mandates that the criteria for a reduction in force be the same for all employees. Employees are not fungible; rather, they have different qualities and responsibilities. To be sure, establishing two or more sets of criteria can lead to challenges, but these challenges are easily answered if the different sets of criteria are well planned and bear a demonstrable relationship to the tasks being measured. For example, nothing is wrong with establishing one set of criteria for production workers, a second set of criteria for management employees, and perhaps even a third set for executive management. Human resources departments often have an urge to develop a "one size fits all" reduction-in-force program, but that policy can undermine effectiveness and lead to unpleasant results.

Once selection criteria are established they should be published and disseminated to all employees. Let employees know how they will be evaluated and let them ask questions. Secrets lead to litigation, but open communication heads it off—as long as the communication is well considered.

Training

The best oversight team and selection criteria in the world are of no value if the managers making selection decisions do not know how to do so correctly. Remarkably, poor decision-making procedures are the rule rather than the exception. Even more remarkably, the problem can be cured relatively simply through manager training. A specialized short course on the reduction in force should be developed and conducted by the oversight team. All managers who are to make layoff selections or who have employees at risk and thus could be consulted by decision-makers should be properly trained.

Training should begin with an explanation of why the reduction in force is occurring. Managers should not simply be able to repeat the stated reason, but should also be required to understand it. Frontline managers will be asked about the reasons for the reduction and it is disappointing and even dangerous for employees to receive garbled, inconsistent answers. If employees perceive a lack of understanding within management, suspicion is fomented. The more suspicion that exists about the company's motivation, the more likely litigation will follow terminations.

Next, the training should explain how the reduction in force will work from an operational standpoint. The concept and duties of the oversight team should be explained, timelines should be provided both verbally and in writing, and decision-makers, as well as managers from whose departments employees will be laid off, should be told what to expect once actual layoffs begin. They should be told to expect emotional responses, including anger, humiliation, denial, and possibly violence. The managers must understand how to deal with each of these emotions. Failure to prepare for these entirely foreseeable reactions tends to make the employer look disorganized and, consequently, unsafe.

The greatest part of training should be spent on explaining and ensuring understanding of the selection criteria. This area is where the majority of reductions in force fall apart, or at least become subject to effective legal challenges. The typical scenario is for managers to be given nebulous criteria such as "potential" and then sent forth to make selections on the basis of their personal understanding, or lack thereof, about what the criteria mean. The end result is that unconsidered and unauthorized criteria actually come into play and inconsistency becomes the rule rather than the exception. When challenged in an age discrimination claim, this type of failure is virtually impossible to explain to a jury's satisfaction.

This outcome does not have to happen if the oversight team has worked diligently at defining the selection criteria. Managers should be provided with copies of definitions and questions should be encouraged; the goal should be to have a complete dialogue on each criterion. It is imperative that all decision-makers be "singing from the same page." This consistency can occur only if questions are asked and answers given. If criteria are to be weighted, multiple examples should be provided to managers. Weighting complicates reductions in force and it really does not add overall value, usually because decision-makers do not understand or simply cannot apply weighted criteria in a meaningful way.

Among the more important training topics are discrimination issues. The oversight team should remind managers that their efforts will be reviewed for signs of discrimination of all types, especially age related. As with the discussion on selection criteria, it is important not to merely speak to the managers about discrimination but rather to have an open dialogue about it. Managers should be given examples of how *subtle discrimination* occurs, and they should be trained that discrimination is not always conscious or overt. It should be realized that most people do not consider themselves to be biased, but they do let their life experiences influence their decisions, often in an unreflective way. This lack of reflection can be a breeding ground for unintentional, yet illegal, discrimination.

The training also should stress the obligations of those people making layoff decisions and the consequences of not following prescribed procedures. Trainers should explain that reductions in force often result in employee challenges and litigation and that every aspect of the reduction program may be reviewed by laid-off employees with a fine-toothed comb for inconsistencies or deviations from the written program. The managers should be advised that if they are the ones to deviate they should expect to be witnesses in litigation and they should be prepared to explain why they did not follow the rules. Although not of a positive nature, this warning usually motivates the decision-makers to take their responsibilities more seriously than they otherwise might and to strictly follow the program. A number of employers use their in-house labor counsel, who is experienced in reduction-in-force age discrimination litigation, to conduct this part of the training. However, this choice arguably creates a risk that your lawyer will become a witness.

The need to closely follow a program does not mean that an appropriate exception can never be made to a reduction-in-force program. However, when an exception occurs it should be documented and approved by both the oversight team and executive management. Exceptions and inconsistencies are the backbone of showing pretext, which means they are the heart of any employment discrimination plaintiff's case. Therefore, exceptions must be limited, explicable, and documented in detail.

The last topic for training should be recall rights, if any, for laid-off employees. Whether to allow laid-off employees to be recalled under a structured program is always the company's decision, but that decision has to be made and announced before layoffs begin. If there are to be no recall rights, the decision-makers must be informed so they do not imply or actually state to laid-off employees that those employees might get their jobs back. Failure to take this action creates unfounded future expectations and increases dissatisfaction when laid-off employees are not recalled as "promised."

"I Didn't Think about That"

The preceding words are not good ones to hear in a courtroom. Nevertheless, these words often are heard in response to cross-examination about historical employee performance documentation, specifically, employee evaluations. If performance is a criterion for a reduction in force, as it almost always is, historical performance documentation absolutely must be reviewed and considered in a meaningful way before making a selection decision. With distressing frequency, decision-makers who have selected employees for layoff ostensibly because of performance testify in court that they never even thought to review the employees' performance evaluations. At best, this admission makes the reduction in force appear disorganized and, at worst, it makes it appear that the selection process was manipulated to the detriment of a certain class of employees, usually those protected by the ADEA.

A typical example is in order. An older, more senior employee is selected for layoff. In court, it is revealed that a younger, less experienced employee, who was retained, had less positive performance evaluations than the terminated employee. That fact, standing alone, is all a jury needs to conclude that the older employee was selected because of age. After all, it normally makes no sense that a documented better performer would be laid off while a younger, less capable person is retained.

Although performance evaluations must be reviewed during the selection process, they do not have to be controlling. Instead, any apparent inconsistency with historical evaluations should be noted and explained by the oversight team in additional documentation. It is suggested also that the oversight team establish a time period for relevant evaluations. The undeniable fact is that an employee's work performance changes over time. The quality of an employee's performance 10 years ago probably has little relevance in assessing current performance levels. Employee performance in the past two to three years generally is important, and that period should be acknowledged by the oversight team as the relevant period of review.

DEMOGRAPHICS AND STATISTICS

Chapter 5 is dedicated entirely to this subject and only a couple of thoughts are offered here. First, understand that demographic and statistical analyses of the affected workforce are potentially critical issues in reductions in force. Next, understand the difference between demographics and statistics. As explained in the statistics chapter, demographics address workforce composition and characteristics, such as gender and age distribution, while statistics are a numerical measure of the probabilities of an occurrence, such as the probability that employees in the protected age group will make up a certain percentage of the total number of persons laid off.

TRANSFERS AND BUMPING

Reductions in force are commonly criticized for last-minute employee transfers. Often, such transfers result from friendships or eleventh-hour realizations that the company's best employees are at the wrong workstation. Regardless of the reason, these transfers always look like what they are in fact—deliberate avoidance of established guidelines. And, when the person whose employment is saved is not within the protected group, these transfers also always serve as a solid foundation for discrimination claims.

It is important for the oversight team to freeze workforce transfers shortly after the decision is made to conduct a reduction in force. Any delay in doing so will look suspicious. This halt also makes it easier for decision-makers to do their job because it lets the company avoid the problem of a moving target. The best way to accomplish this goal is to give notice of the freeze before the criteria, the number of persons to be affected, and the affected departments are announced. Any transfers being processed in the normal course of business should proceed to completion, but once the freeze period begins no transfers should take place in any part of the at-risk workforce.

To be sure, major corporate decisions always suffer from a certain amount of leakage of confidential information. But, absent a major disclosure, it is difficult to criticize the practice of freezing transfers before the reduction in force occurs. If major leaks have occurred and potentially influenced transfer decisions, then all transfers in the relevant period should be reviewed to determine whether they would have been made even in the absence of the leaked information. If not, the transfers probably should be rescinded.

Also, once the employer makes termination selections, any transfers back into the affected segments of the workforce should not be allowed unless openings have occurred through subsequent attrition, disciplinary termination, or some other unforeseen event. Under no circumstances should employees be transferred back into positions that supposedly were eliminated.

Bumping during a reduction in force is a mess. Bumping, or displacing junior employees with more senior employees, is the industrial equivalent of musical chairs. It destroys continuity and makes the reduction practically impossible to administer because the workforce is in a constant state of flux. Bumping also often results in a less desirable workforce being retained. After all, employee happiness is not derived from the notion of moving down the corporate ladder. The best policy for bumping during a reduction in force, unless required by contract or handbook assurances, is to avoid it at all costs. Finally, the employer's decision on whether to allow bumping should be clearly stated in the memorandum defining the selection criteria and addressed in detail during management training.

HIRING DURING AND AFTER REDUCTIONS IN FORCE

For years, the conventional judicial wisdom was that an employer could not hire new employees while conducting a reduction in force. With the prevalence of huge corporate enterprises and diverse work disciplines in diverse locales, courts now are more cognizant that employees are not fungible. As a result, employers generally are safe in hiring during a reduction in force if they can demonstrate that the hiring is for functions distinct from those at risk for layoffs.

Employers who hire and reduce simultaneously from the same group or function must have a very good explanation for their seemingly inconsistent activity because that activity probably will be challenged. The same concept holds true for a reasonable period of time after the reduction in force is completed. Anyone, but especially jurors,

finds it difficult to understand why a company needs to lay off petroleum engineers, for example, only to hire petroleum engineers back
into the same department within three months of the reduction in force.
Certain circumstances may make this necessary, such as dramatic
changes in business climate, new orders from customers, and disciplinary issues, but in those cases the employer should seriously consider
offering former satisfactory employees their jobs back, even if the layoff program did not include recall rights. This recommendation is especially urged if it appears that the job market will bear only younger
applicants for the open positions. Replacements for unexpected vacan-
cies because of terminations or resignations are always appropriate, of
course.

The oversight team should be made aware of all hirings during the
planning and implementation phases of a reduction in force, and it
should continue to monitor new hires for approximately six months
after the layoffs end. Having a clearinghouse for new hires will facili-
tate review of those decisions and may avoid costly errors.

INDEPENDENT ANALYSIS

It is an understatement to say that reductions in force are emotionally charged events and are often confusing for everyone involved.
Commonly, key management members get so close to the action that
they "can't see the forest for the trees." While the oversight team is
extremely helpful in remedying this problem, an outsider's view is
even better. An employer's outside labor counsel should be considered
for this role. The reason is simple. Outside labor counsel will be more
objective and, one hopes, more experienced. Unlike the oversight team
with only one "client" to serve, outside counsel should have many different clients who have been through similar experiences. This variety
will allow an employer to benefit from other companies' experiences,
both good and bad. This suggestion does not mean that counsel should
review each and every decision or employee selection but, rather, only
the general processes to ensure that results are acceptable.

At a minimum, counsel should review the following things:

- Handbooks and policies;

- Published criteria;

- Training outlines and methods;

- Demographics and statistics;

- Exceptions; and

- Any other event unique to the reduction program.

Outside counsel usually should interview several decision-makers to determine how they applied the written processes. Counsel should challenge decision-makers about their reasoning and actions to determine just how strictly they followed the established program. This inquiry is especially necessary when subjective criteria are controlling in the selection process.

Labor counsel also will be able to review certain documentation, such as demographic and statistical studies, for attorney-client privilege and courtroom impact. It also is not uncommon for employers to have outside counsel hire and direct statisticians to analyze the workforce; this action should protect such information from disclosure during litigation.

Outside counsel will not work for free, but employers will find it much more cost effective for an experienced person to identify issues and address them before it is done by an adverse party at trial.

EMPLOYEE COMMUNICATIONS: RIF NOTIFICATION AND EXIT INTERVIEWS

Dignity, professionalism, and candor: exhibiting these traits during a reduction in force is paramount, especially at the end stage of the process. Although these traits are shown through conduct, they also are a form of communication. Just as in other types of relationships, the manner in which reduction-in-force information is communicated will make a significant difference in how employees react and, thus, feel about the company.

This tenet is equally true for both retained and terminated employees. Even those employees who are being retained will have morale issues to address—they want job security, but they also want to work for a company that treats its employees fairly and with dignity. A reduction in force threatens both.

The most successful companies do not keep secrets of this sort from employees. If a reduction in force is going to occur, by all means tell the employees. They can handle it. At this juncture, they need to be told why a reduction in force is going to occur and how selections will be made. Although the reason for a reduction often is known long in advance of its actual occurrence, such as a long-term drop in oil prices and resulting decrease in exploration activities, it needs to be officially confirmed. In contrast, how the reduction process will work is the great mystery for employees. Failing to communicate this information to employees requires them to speculate about the hows and whens, which in turn leads to suspicion and then anger; from these seeds grow lawsuits.

Do not get angry even if employees do, and even if they question your decisions, intelligence, and, perhaps, your heritage. Remember at all times that decision-makers and the oversight team may have to discuss their actions in a courtroom, and those persons do not want to have to explain a loss of composure to a jury.

Advising employees that they have been laid off is always difficult for everyone involved. The following are several rules that will make the notification process and exit interview more tolerable.

- **Notification should always be done in pairs.** This tactic provides the employer with a built-in witness to what transpired and should help avoid the "did too, did not" arguments that often result from one-on-one notifications. It only makes sense, of course, to ensure that the managers delivering the unwelcome news be those who will remain in employment for some time in the future.

- **Be direct.** Tell the employee that he or she has been selected and briefly and truthfully explain why. Agonizing detail is not necessary, but the employee is owed some explanation and he or she will be better able to understand the decision if given one. There is nothing worse than either trying to gloss over a reason for termination or not giving the terminated employee any reason at all. That type of handling is not only insensitive to the employee, but also it is viewed dimly by jurors. Also bear in mind that jurors are angered when a laid-off employee is given a factually incorrect or untruthful reason for termination. Needless to say, that situation should be avoided at all costs.

- **Let the employee talk.** This suggestion does not mean that a debate about the termination should occur; rather, it means the employee should have a brief opportunity to ask questions and express his feelings, no matter how unpleasant this exchange may be. If the employee is inclined to "tell off" the person giving the notification, that person should listen politely but not respond or react. An initial release of anger may be all that is necessary for the employee to move forward in a more productive way.

- **Never allow voices to be raised.** Nothing fruitful comes from shouting and the meeting should be concluded as soon as it begins.

- **Keep the meeting to a reasonable length of time.** Again, this is not a discussion or a debate; nor is it an opportunity for the employee to request reconsideration. It is simply a notification meeting where a simple message is being delivered in a polite and professional way. It is unusual for these initial meetings to take more than 10 to 15 minutes.

- **Determine how the employee will depart the premises.** This recommendation is discussed following this list.

- **Explain any severance benefits.** Examples are outplacement services, benefits continuation, benefit packages, and severance agreements. The employee will not fully absorb the details at that time, and it should be expected that subsequent meetings will be necessary.

- **Identify a person/resource for future contact.** Do not leave laid-off employees in the cold. Give them a number to call or somebody from the oversight team, for example, to contact with questions and concerns and, if appropriate, for references.

- **Thank the employee for his or her service.** No cost is involved and no harm is done in thanking the employee. It may make the employee feel somewhat more valued in a very difficult situation.

- **Document everything.** Everything discussed at the notification meeting should be documented in detail. This action will create a record for subsequent challenges when allegations of promises or assurances, or allegations of admissions of discrimination are made.

- **Do not express sorrow and do not second-guess the decision.** It is not a good idea for the interviewer to state how sorry he is, or how difficult the decision was, and it certainly is never appropriate to suggest that the interviewer would have reached a different decision. Statements like these do not add anything of value from the employer's standpoint and tend only to worsen the effect on the employee.

- **Make no promises.** Under no circumstances should promises of anything be made, unless first proposed in writing by the oversight team. This type of ad-libbing is a sure way to cause problems.

- **Remember the purpose of the meeting.** Always remember that the notification process involves a business event with serious consequences for the employee—how the separation and notification occur often influences whether legal action will follow.

The employer should spend some time planning employee departures. One of the more uncomfortable things an employer must do is to ask laid-off employees to depart the premises. This procedure can be a completely humiliating event for all involved, but especially the employee. Far too often employees with long tenure are asked to gather their belongings and depart the premises immediately. There are times when a supervised, summary departure is necessary, such as when violence is a risk or security is at issue, but those are the exceptions, not the rule. Long-term employees feel that they have "given their life" to the employer and expect to be treated in a more dignified manner. One sure way to get sued is to rob employees of their dignity by, for example, escorting them off the premises in front of their former colleagues.

As a rule of thumb, and depending on individual circumstances, departures should be orchestrated in a way calculated to preserve as much confidentiality, dignity, and privacy as possible. Suggestions include allowing departing employees to come in early or stay after hours to clean their work stations and depart; weekends also are a good time to do this. If the departing employee is truly senior, it is advisable to give him or her the option of deciding how and when co-workers will be told of the termination. The message should be delivered within a reasonable amount of time, but rarely must it be done immediately.

RECAP DOCUMENTATION

One of the final duties of the oversight team should be to prepare a memorandum explaining what has transpired. Great detail is not necessary; however, all steps in the process should be analyzed. Typical report components will include the following:

- Identification of the oversight team members and their day-to-day roles within the organization;

- Explanation of why the reduction in force occurred;

- Identification of selection criteria, with definitions;

- Identification of any restrictions not reflected in the selection criteria, such as limits on transfers, bumping, and recall rights;

- Identification of timelines;

- Explanation of training that was conducted and documentation identifying those in attendance;

- Identification of the employees who were selected and the number of employees who remained;

- Identification of severance benefits offered;

- A brief statement of workforce demographics before and after the reduction (optional);

- A statement of nondiscrimination (mandatory); and

- A statement that the process used was designed only for the instant reduction in force.

It should be self-evident that this document will be an exhibit in any legal action should challenges occur. The document should be prepared accordingly and with complete candor. Needless to say, such a report will go through several drafts before the final product is complete. A single document that encapsulates all that has happened, including when, why, and under whose oversight, is a powerful courtroom tool.

SEVERANCE AND RELEASE AGREEMENTS

Releases of age discrimination claims are addressed fully in chapter 4. A brief mention of severance agreements containing releases, or pledges not to file claims against the company, is made here, however, because releases are commonly used in reductions in force. Also, as explained in the following chapter, the statutory requirements for valid releases of age discrimination claims, especially those arising from mass layoffs, are quite strict. In fact, they are so strict that such releases often are found to be invalid when challenged in court. Great care must be taken in developing severance and release agreement language, as well as the accompanying employee information required under federal law.

CHAPTER 4

SETTLING AGE DISCRIMINATION CLAIMS

When Congress enacted the ADEA it did not address the circumstances under which protected rights or disputed claims could be released. As a result, age discrimination releases for years were subject to the same legal rules as releases of other types of employment discrimination claims. In short, no statutory, administrative, or court oversight existed; instead, the releases were simply private agreements between the employer and the former employee, and the parties were free to decide the terms of an effective release.

In 1990, Congress amended the ADEA with the Older Workers Benefit Protection Act (OWBPA). The OWBPA changed the rules for age discrimination releases by setting strict criteria for releases both of protected rights, such as a release before a claim is actually filed, and disputed claims, such as releases in settlement of pending Equal Employment Opportunity Commission (EEOC) charges or lawsuits.

Congress was provoked into action by the widespread use of releases during mass layoffs in the 1980s. Congress presumed that age discrimination is harder to detect than other types of employment discrimination, and there was concern that releases were being used in situations where employees would not reasonably be expected to know or suspect that age may have played a role in the termination decision. Congress, therefore, concluded that older workers routinely were releasing potential age discrimination claims without being aware of information that would enable them to make an informed decision.

There also was concern about the prevalence of non-negotiable releases and the practice of linking severance benefits to a release of claims. What Congress saw was older workers being confronted on a mass basis with a choice between a termination without benefits or receipt of benefits only upon a complete release of potential claims, including age discrimination claims. The result, to the congressional eye, was that the ADEA was being undermined by employers who routinely were securing either uninformed or coerced releases of protected rights.

From this concern came the OWBPA, which sets forth the minimum requirements for an age discrimination release before it may be considered "knowing and voluntary" under federal law and, thus, binding on the terminated employee. Notwithstanding the congressional focus on mass layoffs, OWBPA requirements ultimately were extended to all types of age discrimination releases, including those by employees terminated during reductions in force and those by individually terminated employees, releases by employees with existing legal claims and those who do not believe their rights have been violated, and even releases by employees who leave their employment voluntarily.

Employers should be mindful of the OWBPA's extremely specific release requirements and should be aware that courts interpret those requirements strictly, that is, contrary to employer interests. In the event of a dispute about OWBPA compliance, the employer has the burden of proving compliance.

For these reasons, the human resource professional should have a good working knowledge of OWBPA requirements.

WHAT THE LAW COVERS

The OWBPA addresses four different release scenarios: (1) a release by an involuntarily terminated employee who has not filed an EEOC charge or lawsuit; (2) releases by employees involuntarily terminated pursuant to group reductions in force and who have not filed age claims; (3) releases in settlement of disputed claims, either pending EEOC charges or civil actions; and (4) releases by employees who have voluntarily opted to sever employment pursuant to an incentive program.

The good news is that most of the requirements in all four situations are the same. The common requirements are as follows:

1. The release must be part of an agreement between an employee and the employer that is "written in a manner calculated to be understood" by the employee or the average employee eligible for a reduction in force;

2. The release must specifically refer to rights or claims protected under the ADEA;

3. The release must address only rights or claims that arose on or before the date it is executed; that is, the employee cannot release the employer for any future acts of age discrimination;

4. The employee can effectively release rights or claims only in exchange for something of value to which he is not already entitled by virtue of the employment relationship; and

5. The employee must be advised in writing to consult with an attorney before executing the release.

These requirements are simple enough and employers usually satisfy them in securing releases.

It should be emphasized, however, that the OWBPA specifically states that a release must be "written in a manner calculated to be understood" by the employee. Releases cannot be very long or choked with legalese. Instead, release documents should be brief and the language used should be plain; the more "conversational" the release, the better, and this language can be written without sacrificing effectiveness. The educational level and general sophistication of the individual employee or average employee should be taken into account and the release modified accordingly. A release also should say that the employees understand the language of the release and its effect, specifically including that they are releasing any age discrimination rights or disputed claims they may have as of the date they execute it.

Employees must also receive something of value to which they are not already entitled. For example, giving terminated employees something to which they may already be entitled as part of a severance program or pursuant to an existing policy, such as accrued sick and vacation pay, will not support an effective release. Employees must receive something of value over and above anything that they would receive upon termination even if they did not execute a release of claims. In those situations in which a standard severance package is in place, for example, the employer will have to offer employees enhanced severance pay to purchase effective releases.

Some employers may balk at the thought of advising departing employees to consult with counsel, but they do so at their own peril. Every release of age discrimination rights or claims should include a simple, prominent statement near the end of the document to the effect that the employee has been advised to consult with an attorney before executing it. A release need only state, "You are hereby advised to consult with an attorney," to satisfy this requirement. The employee's opportunity to seek legal advice is crucial to a knowledgeable assessment of his or her legal rights. Therefore, that opportunity is central to congressional purpose in enacting the OWBPA, and employers must strictly observe the requirement.

THE CONSIDERATION PERIOD

The next requirement in all four release scenarios is that employees must be given adequate time to consider their releases before executing them: (1) an individual employee who does not have a pending claim must be given "at least 21 days" in which to consider a release; (2) employees terminated during group reductions in force, or who leave voluntarily via group incentive programs must be given "at least 45 days" to consider a release; and (3) an employee executing a release in settlement of an existing EEOC charge or lawsuit must be given "a reasonable period of time" to consider a release.

Although the OWBPA is silent on the point, employers are wise to treat these "consideration periods" as being triggered only upon an employee's actual receipt of the written release agreement. It is not enough that an employee simply be told what the terms of a release will be. Also, a release should include a clear statement that the employee has been given the appropriate amount of time to consider the release agreement.

Some employers are under the mistaken impression that the consideration period must pass completely before a release may be executed. In fact, an employee may execute a release before the applicable consideration period has expired. The OWBPA only requires that an employee be given adequate time to consider a release. Nothing in the statute prevents an employee from accepting a release agreement earlier.

What a "reasonable period of time" may be in the context of a release in settlement of an existing claim is not well defined. It will, no doubt, depend on the circumstances. Generally, however, a reasonable period of time will be considerably less than the 21- or 45-day consideration periods. Obviously, an employee who has filed a claim already is aware of his or her rights, believes they have been violated, and probably is represented by an attorney. As long as the employer did not coerce the employee, and the release agreement specifically states that the employee was given a reasonable period of time in which to consider the agreement, the OWBPA should be satisfied.

THE REVOCATION PERIOD

Those employees who do not have pending claims must be given "at least 7 days" after they execute a release to change their mind and revoke it. The OWBPA states that a release "shall not become effective or enforceable until the revocation period has expired." Therefore, unlike the consideration period, the revocation period cannot be waived by an employee. Congress, in effect, has provided an out for the employee who has buyer's remorse after releasing age-related rights.

The law does not require an employee to be paid before the revocation period has expired and, obviously, it makes sense to hold off payment until then. In the event an employee is paid before the revocation period expires and then revokes the release simply because of a change of mind, the money should be returned to the employer—assuming the employee still has it. Some employers use a separate document titled "Acknowledgment of Non-Revocation," which an employee must execute after expiration of the revocation period and return to the employer before payment of any money.

REQUIREMENTS FOR GROUP TERMINATION AND INCENTIVE PROGRAMS

If a release is requested in connection with a group program, either an involuntary reduction in force or a voluntary group incentive program, two additional and more problematic requirements exist for valid releases.

Eligible Employees

First, at the beginning of the consideration period all employees eligible for a group program must be informed in writing, and "in a manner calculated to be understood by the average individual eligible to participate," as to (1) "any class, unit, or group of individuals" covered by the program; (2) any "eligibility factors" for the program; and (3) any time limits applicable to the program.

Initially, an employer must publicly identify the targeted employee groups. Circumstances will dictate what employees must be told. It may be that all employees in the company are subject to the group program, or only a certain division, facility, or group of departments may be affected. In a voluntary group incentive program, such as an early retirement program, only employees in a certain age group may be eligible, that is, affected.

The eligibility factors that employers must disclose are simply those characteristics that qualify employees for a group program. Examples of eligibility factors that could apply in an involuntary group program, such as a reduction in force, include employees whose jobs have been eliminated, who are offered transfers requiring relocation, or who have had a reduction in base pay. Although somewhat counterintuitive, the OWBPA refers to these as "eligibility factors" even in the context of an involuntary program because, as shown by the latter two examples, in some situations employees may have the option of remaining employed under changed circumstances or terminating employment in accordance with the group program.

Examples of eligibility factors that could apply in a voluntary group program, such as an early retirement program, include employees of a certain minimum age and who have a minimum number of years of service.

The time limit requirement is straightforward. Employers must inform employees of any "window" for volunteering for a program, or of any closing date for selection of employees in an involuntary program.

Demographic Information

The second requirement is that eligible employees must be informed in writing and in a manner calculated to be understood by the average individual eligible to participate about the job titles and ages of all individual employees eligible or selected for the group program, and the ages of all employees in the "same job classification or organizational unit" who are not eligible or selected for the same program.

This requirement often causes problems for employers. In truly mass layoff situations, compiling this type of information can be extremely time-consuming and costly. Furthermore, the consequences of failing to compile accurate data are severe. At the very least, any releases could be invalidated; at the worst, additional claims could be filed against an employer for fraud.

The employer should note that the OWBPA specifies the content but not the format for the required information. Two relatively simple formats for communicating the required information to employees are as follows. First, an employer may simply create two separate lists of employees organized by job title, and also including ages (or dates of birth) and geographical location (or "organizational unit"): the first list would identify all employees eligible or selected for the program, and the second list would identify all employees in the same job titles or organizational units who are not eligible or selected for the program.

A second type of format would be a simple chart or matrix, with affected job titles and locations alphabetized along the left margin and employee ages designated along the top. The employer would simply chart the number of employees with particular job titles and ages. See Table 1.

Table 1. Example of Chart to Fulfill OWBPA Requirement

	...	35	36	37	38	39	40	41	42	...
Accountant I		4	1	2		1				
Engineer II		1		1	2		4		1	
Secretary III				1		3	1	1	4	

A set of charts could be created for each geographic location or organizational unit; the first chart would identify affected employees, and the second would identify unaffected or retained employees in the same job titles. Each chart should be designated with easily understood titles.

One final note about this requirement for valid releases of age discrimination claims. It is not necessary for an employer to summarize the demographic information provided; indeed, it may be statistically misleading to do so. Nor is an employer required to make the demographic information readily susceptible to any statistical analysis that an employee or his attorney may want to attempt. It is only necessary to provide the required information accurately.

As difficult and costly as this last requirement may be, it is at least consistent with congressional purpose. As noted, Congress's primary purpose in enacting the OWBPA was to provide employees terminated during mass layoffs with sufficient information and the time to consider it so they could make knowledgeable releases of potential age claims. The requirement that demographic information be provided in mass layoffs comes closest to satisfying this goal. It allows the terminated employee to make a rough comparison of the ages of employees severing employment with those in the same job classifications who remain. The comparison can be made by specific job title or on an overall basis. Bear in mind, however, that such simple comparisons do not constitute valid statistical analyses and, thus, they do not tend to prove or disprove that age was a factor in the decision-making process.

MINIMUM REQUIREMENTS

The OWBPA sets forth only the minimum requirements for valid releases of age-related rights and claims. A release may not be considered to be knowing and voluntary unless at a minimum all statutory requirements are met. This principle leaves open the possibility that a release that satisfies all statutory requirements nevertheless may be held invalid. This type of ruling could occur when an employer satisfied the letter of the law as far as statutory requirements, but misled an employee into executing a release by giving him or her a false reason for that specific termination.

For example, in a mass layoff an employer may satisfy all OWBPA requirements on the surface in securing a release of claims. But, if the employer deliberately misrepresented the facts, saying that an employee's position was eliminated when it actually was reassigned to a younger employee, the terminated employee may have a fraudulent inducement claim that would allow him or her to revoke his or her release long after the revocation period has expired and to sue for age discrimination.

THE RISK OF NONCOMPLIANCE

In 1998, the United States Supreme Court held that a release of age claims that does not fully comply with OWBPA requirements is of no effect. In that case the employee was given the option of either improving her job performance during the coming year or accepting a voluntary arrangement for her severance. The employer gave her a packet of information about the severance agreement and gave her 14 days to consider her options, during which she consulted with attorneys. The employee then accepted the severance package and executed a release in which she agreed to "waive, settle, release, and discharge any and all claims" she may have had against her former employer.

The Supreme Court held that the release did not comply with OWBPA in at least three respects, including that (1) the employer did not give the employee enough time to consider her options, that is, she should have had 21 days instead of 14; (2) the employer did not give the employee 7 days after she signed her release to change her mind; and (3) the release made no specific reference to claims arising under the ADEA.

The employer argued that its admitted failure to comply with the OWBPA was not prejudicial to the employee and, moreover, that it did not matter because the employee had not tried to revoke her release, although she believed her rights had been violated, and she had not returned the money she had been paid for her release. The employer argued that by her actions the employee had "ratified," that is, agreed to abide by, her release although it was defective under the OWBPA.

The Supreme Court rejected the employer's arguments and held simply that releases of age discrimination claims that do not comply with all applicable OWBPA requirements are invalid and, thus, of no effect.

The Supreme Court also held that an employee who executes a release defective under the OWBPA does not have to return the money she was paid before suing her former employer for age discrimination. In other words, where the employer fails to comply with OWBPA requirements, an employee may sue for age discrimination notwithstanding her execution of the release, and she can bankroll her lawsuit with the very money the employer paid for her release.

It is clear that courts will interpret OWBPA requirements strictly and that any defect, no matter its seeming insignificance, will invalidate a release of age claims. Furthermore, the employer will be unable to demand return of the money it paid for the release prior to any related litigation. Failure to comply with the OWBPA brings harsh consequences; indeed, the consequences of noncompliance may be so harsh that it will cause employers to question whether releases of age discrimination claims are worth the effort, especially in mass layoff situations.

CHAPTER 5

STATISTICS AND DEMOGRAPHICS

The subject of statistics usually does one of three things to persons, including judges and jurors: it intimidates them, it puts them to sleep, or, most commonly, it confuses them. The latter reaction in particular makes it important to have a basic grasp of how statistical analysis comes into play in employment discrimination cases. Historically, both litigants and the courts have fallen prey to ill-founded statistical analyses; this statement is true both for plaintiffs and defendants, but generally it has been to the employer's detriment. A basic understanding of how and why statistics are used in these cases and a recognition of the recurring problems associated with their use will better prepare the employer to both make and defend its case.

THE DIFFERENCE BETWEEN DEMOGRAPHICS AND STATISTICS

The most fundamental point to be made about the use and misuse of statistics in employment discrimination cases is that demographics and statistics are not the same. Demographics simply describe and classify certain characteristics, such as gender and age, of a defined workforce. For example, a demographic profile of an employer's workforce may show that on a given date 60 of 100 employees, or 60 percent of the workforce, were under age 40, and 40 of 100 employees, or 40 percent of the workforce, were age 40 or older. Workforce demographics might also show that during a reduction in force, 4 out of 10 employees chosen for termination, or 40 percent, were age 40 or older.

A statistic, in employment discrimination cases, is a numerical conclusion about the chance that a certain selection result will occur if an employer's decision-making process is random, that is, unbiased. A statistic might show, for example, that if an employer's reduction-in-force selection process is unbiased and if 40 percent of the workforce is age 40 or older, the likelihood that its decisions would result in 4 out of 10 terminated employees being age 40 or older is approximately 95 percent, or quite likely. In other words, a simple statistical analysis, without consideration of other factors, might lead to the conclusion that "the odds are high" that a certain result can be expected from an unbiased selection process.

In summary, demographics reveal facts about the composition of a workforce. Demographics, however, do not provide information about the probability that a certain workforce will have a particular composition at a given point in time. Statistics, in contrast, may be used to convey information about the likelihood that a certain workforce composition will result from unbiased selection processes.

A substantial problem, especially for employers, results when a judge or jury treats a simple demographic observation as if it were a statistical conclusion. Consider the following illustration. Suppose an employer decides it must reduce its workforce by 100 employees. The employer's workforce is composed of persons between the ages of 18 and 70, with 50 percent of the total workforce age 40 or older. When termination decisions are announced, 70 of the 100 terminated employees are age 40 or older. A demographic analysis would permit us only to observe and conclude that 70 percent of the terminated persons were in a particular age grouping, that is, age 40 and older, and no more. However, someone who assumes that a different distribution of ages among terminated employees should have been reached based on workforce demographics might be tempted to treat the demographic observation as a statistical analysis and to conclude that the employer's selection process was biased against older employees.

Such a conclusion would be inappropriate, although it is often the one reached. For example, the entire workforce may not have been at risk of termination, but only a portion of it, such as people in certain positions with a different age distribution than the total workforce. If approximately 70 percent of the at-risk workforce consisted of employees age 40 or older, then a statistical analysis, after consideration of the appropriate factors, would show that the likelihood that an unbiased selection process would result in 70 percent of terminated employees being age 40 or older is approximately 95 percent. In other words, the actual outcome should have been expected.

Remember that statistics and demographics provide different types of information about a workforce. Although they often interrelate and often are used in conjunction with each other, do not confuse the two or allow an adversarial employee to blur the distinctions between these very different types of analyses.

THE LIMITED VALUE OF STATISTICS IN DISPARATE TREATMENT CASES

The value of statistical analysis in disparate treatment cases is limited because it tries to prove a person's subjective state of mind through purely quantitative analysis. For example, although a decision-maker who has selected a group of employees for termination denies he was motivated by unlawful age bias, at trial a former employee may be allowed to introduce a "statistical analysis" of those terminations in order to show that they reflect a pattern of age-biased decisions. That showing, in turn, would serve as the foundation for the employee's argument that his own termination must have resulted from intentional age bias.

However, an obvious incompatibility lies between what a person may have thought about a specific employee on a certain date and a numerical analysis of that person's decisions at other times about other employees with different personal and employment-related characteristics. Even assuming some pattern of conduct could be shown with a statistical analysis, it does not prove that a person acted in accordance on a specific occasion. Statistical analysis simply cannot account for all the factors, influences, and nuances that drive the human decision-making process; nor can it differentiate between individual employment decisions based on qualitative, or non-numerical, factors.

Statistical analysis is better suited for disparate impact cases, where it is not necessary to prove unlawful intent. Instead, under that theory of liability, it must be demonstrated only that an employment policy or practice had an adverse impact on a protected group. Numbers can accurately reflect such patterns in some circumstances. As noted, however, the trend has been for the courts to find that disparate impact theory is not a proper basis for a lawsuit under the ADEA.

Many technical problems are also associated with statistical analyses in employment discrimination cases, as discussed below. In short, because no commonly agreed-upon analytical method exists, because the employment data being reviewed may be incomplete or susceptible to widely varying interpretations, and because an analysis may be significantly affected by the preconceptions or misconceptions of the person making it, the conclusions drawn may be wrong.

THE LIMITED VALUE OF STATISTICS IN AGE DISCRIMINATION CASES

The use of statistical analysis in age discrimination cases is particularly problematic. Studies by occupational analysts show that, standing alone, surveys of the older employee population in any workforce often will produce results that make it appear that older employees are treated less favorably than younger employees. There are several explanations for this phenomenon. First, according to industrial research, older employees are more likely to voluntarily exit the active workforce than younger employees. Research shows, for example, that older employees voluntarily quit their employment because of illness or retirement more often than younger employees. In other words, certain phenomena affect all workforces and tend to have a greater negative impact on older persons' continued employment. As a result, if a numerical analysis of an employer's workforce reflects fewer older persons than would normally be expected, it could be the result of factors beyond the employer's control rather than unlawful age bias. If these types of demographic phenomena are not identified and controlled for in a statistical analysis, the conclusions drawn will be inaccurate and misleading, with significant adverse consequences for an unwary employer.

Industrial research also shows that older persons are more likely to remain unemployed than younger persons after an employment separation, regardless of the reason. Older persons often are overqualified for the type of entry-level employment that is most plentiful in the job market. Older persons' wage expectations also are higher, on average, than younger persons' because of prior work experience. Older persons also may be at risk of extended unemployment because they lack the current technical skills sought by employers. These types of employment characteristics, if actually present, may be lawful bases for employment decisions.

If a supposed statistical analysis fails to—or is unable to—account for these kinds of lawful explanations for an employer's workforce composition, then the analysis is evidence of nothing. Notwithstanding these significant limitations, however, the parties in age discrimination cases routinely engage in some debased form of statistical analysis, and courts and juries routinely are influenced by it.

VALID STATISTICAL ANALYSES

The first criterion for a valid statistical analysis is that it actually be a statistical analysis, as opposed to a mere demographic-based conclusion, as explained above. There are four additional basic criteria for a valid statistical analysis; each is addressed in turn.

The analysis must use a statistical model that correlates with the manner in which the challenged decisions were made. Federal courts have come to recognize that a statistical analysis must be based on a model that mirrors the manner in which the employer's decisions were made and that "tests" a population of employees that is similar to the plaintiff-employee in employment characteristics, such as job classification, educational and skills level, experience in position and grade, and identity of supervisors as it relates to the selection processes. It makes no sense, for example, to analyze how many employees age 40 or older were individually terminated by Supervisor A between the months of March and June in a given year if the act of unlawful discrimination alleged by the plaintiff-employee was made by

Supervisor B during a layoff that occurred in December of the same year.

Likewise, relevant evidence likely cannot be gleaned from a statistical analysis performed on Supervisor B's promotion decisions made over the course of a five-year period from a changing pool of candidates when those challenged decisions are analyzed as if they were made simultaneously from a static pool of candidates.

The results of a statistical analysis can be manipulated merely by choosing to include or exclude certain employee populations in the test being conducted. Manipulation of data most often occurs in analyses of large reductions in force; the choice of employee populations will virtually dictate the outcome of the analysis in those cases.

Therefore, whether considering for use or criticizing a statistical analysis, an employer should review the following questions:

- Are the employees accurately counted?

- Are the populations of employees chosen for analysis the proper ones for comparison?

- Are the employees who make up the comparison populations similarly situated in educational and skills levels, job titles, and other factors relevant to the employer's decision-making process?

- Are the employer's decisions properly modeled; for instance, are separate decisions treated as separate events, and are decisions tested in the proper sequence?

- Are the effects of the employer's successive decisions on the available sample population taken into account?

If affirmative answers cannot be given to these questions, the statistical analysis under scrutiny should be considered suspect.

The statistical analysis must be based on an analytical technique that is appropriate for the type of data available. A valid statistical analysis will (1) determine what would be the expected outcome of an employer's decision-making process, assuming the process was unbiased; (2) compare the expected outcome with the actual outcome of the employer's decision-making process; and (3) determine the likelihood that the actual outcome of the selection process would have occurred given the assumption that the employer's selection process was unbiased.

Many kinds of analytical techniques may be used to make these comparisons and determinations. The technique that will be best suited for a particular case depends on the decision-making process at issue, the number of employment decisions made by the employer, the size of the sample populations, and the availability of accurate data for use in the analysis.

For example, the *binomial technique* analyzes an employer's decision-making process using the number of decisions made by the employer, the percentage of employees available for selection by the employer who are members of the protected age group, and the total number of employees in the at-risk workforce population. The binomial technique permits a statistician to report, in terms of standard deviations, the likelihood that a certain number of employees in the legally protected class would have been selected by the employer assuming the selection process was random—a characteristic that rarely, if ever, exists in employment decisions.

The binomial technique is appropriate only if accurate demographic information is available about the composition of the population of employees available for selection by the employer, the number of employer selections is known and is relatively large, and the size of the population of employees in the at-risk pool also is sufficiently large. Also, for the results of a binomial technique analysis to be valid, the employees available for selection by the employer must be similarly attractive to the employer; that is, they must be similarly situated in employment qualifications.

The binomial technique does not account for changes in the composition of the pool of employees available for selection as the employer's decisions are made and employees are drawn out of the at-risk population. Thus, the binomial technique may be validly relied on only when the population of employees available for selection is so large that the employer's selection process inappreciably affects the distribution of legally protected employees within the selection population.

When a statistical analysis should correct for the mathematical results of an employer's selections on the distribution of legally protected employees in the selection-available population, the analytical technique most often used is the *hypergeometric technique*. This technique corrects for the results of the employer's decisions on the population of employees eligible for selection and may be used to analyze an employer's decision-making when the sample of employees available for selection is relatively small.

When the employees available for selection belong to more than two mutually exclusive groups, such as when the employees are of varied races or national origin and a statistician is seeking to test the probability of an outcome of an employer's decision-making for more than one of these legally protected groups simultaneously, the *chi square technique* is appropriate. To be valid, the chi square technique requires large sample populations. When sample populations are small, statisticians often choose to rely on a technique known as the *Fisher's exact test*, a statistical test used with small samples to compute the probability of an outcome.

It is not necessary for an employer to know about or fully understand all the various types of analytical techniques to be able to gain a sense of whether a chosen analytical technique is appropriate. To determine whether an analytical technique is appropriate, an employer need only keep the following two questions in mind:

- Does the available data conform with the requirements of the particular analytical technique being used (as described above)?

- Is there an analytical technique better suited for the kind of data available?

The statistical analysis must test the appropriate size sample population. As may be seen from the preceding discussion, the size of the sample populations of employees greatly influences the analytical process. The size of a sample population is important for many reasons, but three reasons are primary. First, all analytical techniques require numerous employer selections and a relatively large population of employees. Except in rare cases, no valid statistical conclusion can be drawn based on 1 or 2 or even 10 employer selections out of a population of 10 or 20 employees.

Second, the effort to find a sufficiently large population of employees for testing often causes a party to disregard whether the employees included in the analysis actually possess the requisite characteristics of similar job positions, educational and skills levels, and experience. Another factor that may be overlooked or disregarded is whether the decisions being analyzed bore any relationship to one another, such as whether they were part of a larger decision-making process or were simply a series of unrelated, individually made decisions. The need for sufficiently large sample populations may lead to the consideration of inappropriate or inaccurate data and thus introduce significant bias in the statistical analysis.

Although large sample populations usually are necessary for a valid statistical analysis, accurate data may not exist or be available. Consequently, in some circumstances it may not be possible to perform a valid statistical analysis on the employer decisions at issue.

The statistical analysis must correct for error. Even when the appropriate sample populations are chosen, an appropriate analytical technique is used, and the analysis is properly modeled, substantial error may nevertheless occur if the analyst has made no correction for factors that may falsely indicate bias in the statistical results. One such source of error is prevalent in statistical analyses made in age discrimination cases, especially those arising from reductions in force. This source of error is referred to as *Aggregation Bias*, and it can be easily demonstrated.

For example, assume that an employer makes termination decisions in two separate reductions in force occurring six months apart. In the first reduction, there are 1,000 employees in the job titles from which termination selections are made, and 300 of those 1,000 employees, or 30 percent, are age 40 or older. Assume all candidates for the reduction have similar qualifications. In the first reduction, 100 employees are chosen for termination and 30 of those 100 employees, or 30 percent, are age 40 or older. This percentage of protected-age employees is what one would most likely expect to be selected in a random selection process.

In the second reduction, 300 employees are in the at-risk population; 200 of those 300 employees, or 66 percent, are age 40 or older, and all the candidates are similarly qualified. In the second reduction, 100 employees are chosen for termination and, of those, 66, or 66 percent, are age 40 or older. This is again the expected number assuming the selection process is random. No inference of discriminatory intent can be drawn here, either.

Now, assume that a statistician analyzes the employer's decision-making process by treating both reductions in force as though they occurred simultaneously, that is, as a single event, rather than occurring six months apart. Under this analysis, 1,300 employees are in the at-risk population, 500 of whom, or 38 percent, are age 40 or older. The statistician, treating the reductions as if they were one event, considers that 200 employees have been chosen for termination. The statistician would expect, based on the percentage of workers in the protected age group, that 38 percent, or 76, of the 200 terminated employees would be age 40 or older if the employer's selection process had been random. In fact, the employer actually selected a total of 96 protected-age employees for termination during the reductions.

The statistician would conclude that a significant disparity exists between the expected result and the actual result, and he may attribute the disparity to unlawful age bias. Yet, in actuality, if the statistical analysis had been correctly modeled to conform to the employer's decision-making process, the properly drawn conclusions would be contrary.

Aggregation bias is only one of several errors that may invalidate a statistical analysis. Error may also arise when an employer's objective selection criteria, such as a certain educational or seniority level, are not taken into account in the analysis. Also, analytical error may arise when "self-selecting" employees, such as those voluntarily resigning or taking early retirement, are not removed from the sample population. Sources of potential error like these and others must be identified and controlled for before a statistical analysis has any validity.

STATISTICALLY BASED CONCLUSIONS OF UNLAWFUL DISCRIMINATION

Even a properly modeled and controlled statistical analysis cannot prove or disprove that unlawful discriminatory intent existed in a challenged decision-making process. The only valid, scientifically proper conclusion that may be drawn from a proper statistical analysis is the likelihood (reported as a mathematical probability) that the observed outcome of an employer's selection process would have occurred given the assumption that the selection process was unbiased. No statistical expert, however, can legitimately conclude that an employer's selection process was intentionally biased against any protected group of employees, even given a notable observed disparity in the results of the employer's selection process. Many courts, nevertheless, allow so-called statistical experts to do just that.

One type of erroneous statistical conclusion that is routinely made in analyzing employment decisions is referred to as the *transposition fallacy*. This error is committed as follows. A statistical analysis shows, for example, that assuming an employer's selection process is unbiased, the likelihood that a particular outcome will result is only 5 percent. This statistical conclusion, of course, means that although the outcome may be statistically unlikely, it is nevertheless presumed to be a possible result of unbiased selection procedures. Indeed, in every statistical test or measurement it is expected that there will be statistically significant deviations from the mean. In nature, as with all human endeavor, identical results are not obtained every time, even from processes that indisputably are unbiased. Therefore, simply because a result may be statistically unlikely says nothing about the probability that it was the result of a biased selection process.

In the employment context, however, it is frequently concluded that if the likelihood that the actual outcome was the result of an unbiased process is only 5 percent, then there is a 95 percent probability that it was the result of a biased, that is, unlawful, process. In other words, it is concluded that there is a 95 percent chance that the employer's process was discriminatory.

The error of this type of conclusion is illustrated by the following example. If a large group of persons each flipped an identical coin 100 times, it would be expected that most of them would have a fairly even distribution between heads and tails, that is, most persons would have between 45 and 55 "heads." However, it also should be expected that if the group is large enough, a certain percentage of the group will have statistically significant disparity in their results; that is, some of them will have between 55 and 65 "heads." Although the likelihood of that disparity may be relatively small, it still is a normal, expected occurrence. More important, the likelihood of a disparity occurring says nothing about the likelihood that it was obtained by cheating, that is, that it was obtained by introducing bias into the process. Nevertheless, the likelihood of a disparity often is incorrectly transposed with the likelihood that it was the result of nonrandom, or biased, processes. Instead of making the quick and easy mistake of the "transposition fallacy," nonstatistical information should be gathered and analyzed in order to understand what caused the disparity.

Employers must recognize that statistically significant disparities may exist in their workforces; in fact, the larger the employer the more likely that significant workforce disparities will exist in specific departments or job classifications. But workforce disparities are not necessarily indicative of biased decision-making processes. Instead, disparities can and often do result from unbiased decisions. The task for employers who either discover or are alleged to have significant workforce disparities is to understand whether the cause was lawful. That discovery can be achieved only by analyzing nonstatistical information.

CHAPTER 6

COMMON PROBLEMS TO AVOID

All employment decisions, especially termination decisions, should be made with a clear recognition of the real possibility that the decision will be scrutinized topside and bottom by outsiders—including lawyers, fair employment agencies, judges, and a jury. The EEOC is under a statutory mandate to review employment decisions that an employee challenges under one of the federal statutes that the agency is responsible for enforcing; parallel state fair employment agencies have similar responsibilities. (See chapter 10 regarding the administrative process.) Beyond that, the decision is certainly subject to review by lawyers, courts, and juries.

An employer should give much care, therefore, to the surrounding facts and circumstances before taking an adverse employment action toward a protected-age employee. Although such facts may not be part of the employer's decision-making process, the case may appear otherwise to some person or group reviewing the decision from the outside. And, indeed, the existence of certain facts may actually delay or change an employer's decision about a protected-age employee.

This chapter addresses certain types of employment-related facts that routinely cause problems for employers in age discrimination claims and recommends how employers can avoid them.

MERIT RAISES AND PERFORMANCE EVALUATIONS

A recurring difficulty encountered in defending age discrimination claims stems from improper use of employee merit raises and evaluations. A common example is for an employer to rely on an employee's supposedly unsatisfactory performance as the basis for an employment decision, only to be confronted by outside counsel, the EEOC, or, worse, a questioner at a trial with contrary employee performance evaluations or a history of the employee's merit raises. An all-too-common question faced by an employer is the following: why, if the plaintiff was as bad as the employer says he was, do his evaluations and salary history reflect that he was a "good" or "above average" employee?

Most assuredly, if formal evaluations are used they should be done uniformly, accurately, and in a timely manner. They also should relate, at least in part, to objective criteria that are job related. Further, evaluations should be honest and should relate to the real world. If an employee is a poor performer, then the evaluation should reflect that. Often, employers rank an employee as "good" when he or she is, in fact, a poor performer. The justification for debasing the evaluation system almost always is that other employees are rated "excellent," and by comparison a "good" evaluation is really not very good. It should be unnecessary to say that it is difficult to convince the EEOC or a jury that an employee who is rated as "good" is anything but "good."

When an apparent inconsistency exists between actual employee performance and the employer's records of performance, an employer must do two basic things: first, the decision-makers must be aware of the inconsistency; and, second, they must be prepared to explain it plausibly. It is surprising how often employers of all kinds and sizes simply fail to review personnel records when disciplining or terminating protected employees. A basic step in human resource procedure should be to review personnel records before implementing significant adverse decisions against any employee, but especially legally protected employees.

Next, when an inconsistency exists, it must be explained. Often, identifying an explanation is simple enough to do. For example, a significant gap in time, perhaps 6 to 12 months, may have occurred between the last formal evaluation and the onset of performance problems. Or, the employee's job title, duties, or supervisor may have changed since his or her last evaluation. Also, the practice may be for all employees to receive "merit raises" as a matter of course, and the raises are best explained as cost of living raises, which are not really indicative of quality of performance. If no apparent or plausible explanation can be made for the discrepancy, however, the company should recognize the need to reevaluate the decision.

"Outsiders" have a hard time reconciling an employer's claims of poor job performance with contrary performance evaluations and salary histories. Such outside parties are far more likely to think or find that an employer's asserted reasons for a challenged employment decision are a pretext for age discrimination when those reasons are contradicted by the employer's own personnel and business records.

INCONSISTENCY BETWEEN THE STATED AND ACTUAL REASONS FOR AN EMPLOYMENT ACTION

One simple rule that is often overlooked when dealing with problem employees is the rule of honesty. If an employment problem exists, it should be confronted directly; it should not be avoided or handled in a less-than-candid manner. This rule culminates with an honest statement of the reason for discipline or termination. In short, the official reason, that is, the one recorded on an employer's personnel action notice, must be the actual reason for the adverse decision.

Often, employers are reluctant to sit down with an employee and discuss problems that are affecting that employee's performance. Even when the employee's performance has become intolerable, many employers look for a way to terminate the employee, while attempting to avoid the real issue. In those circumstances, terminations that actually are "for cause" are recharacterized as reductions in force or voluntary resignations. If a fair employment agency or a jury recognizes a discrepancy between the stated and the actual reason for a challenged employment decision, then it will be suspicious of everything else the employer has to say about that decision.

Employment problems also should be dealt with promptly and fairly. Problems delayed do not go away; instead, they grow and multiply. Further, whatever discipline is administered should fit the crime, so to speak. For example, all too often an employer will tolerate an employee's misconduct for too long and then become fed up and seize upon a relatively insignificant event as a basis for termination. Later attempts to draw in and connect all the other instances of poor performance are unconvincing, especially if the only stated reason for termination was the seemingly insignificant event.

The difficulties that arise from not quickly and frankly addressing performance or other employment problems are illustrated by the following hypothetical situation. Employee Jones has a disagreeable demeanor. He is confrontational and argumentative. Let us assume that he is in a protected class—he is over age 40—and that Jones has work performance problems. His supervisor has had no formal training in personnel matters. The supervisor has learned that life is much easier if he overlooks the work performance problems of Jones and ignores his unacceptable conduct. There is a rational basis for the supervisor's decision; confrontations with Jones not only are unpleasant, but also they distract the supervisor from what he perceives to be his primary job—maximizing production. Even Jones's performance evaluations do not reflect his shortcomings. The supervisor has found it easier to mark Jones as an "average" performer than to go through the hassle of explaining notations of substandard performance to Jones and then justifying them to those higher in the organization.

Finally, however, the supervisor has had enough. On the fateful day, Jones arrives at work five minutes late, and he is summarily terminated. Jones has given his supervisor a quick and easy basis for acting, and the supervisor seizes upon it.

Jones sues, asserting that he was terminated because of his age. The employer's defense is that although the precipitating event might have been a minor instance of tardiness, it was the proverbial straw that broke the camel's back. Unfortunately, however, Jones's personnel file contains no record of the accumulating misconduct that made the final straw so intolerable and understandable. Although the supervisor can try to describe in the courtroom how unpleasant Jones really was, the sterile courtroom environment makes it difficult to recreate the work environment. The supervisor's tolerant attitude not only has created a situation that will make the termination difficult to defend, but it probably created personnel problems that extend beyond Jones.

This distressingly common fact pattern shows why unacceptable performance should result in immediate counseling and appropriate disciplinary action. If the employee does not improve, then progressive discipline should be instituted with the employee ultimately terminated if necessary. Even though Jones may have been a pain in the neck, something seems unfair about terminating an employee because he was five minutes late for work. When all is said and done, all the employer will be able to present by way of a defense is that Jones was unproductive and unpleasant at unspecified times, notwithstanding that his personnel file does not so reflect. Undoubtedly, Jones will contend that the company was out to get rid of him because of his age and that the reasons offered by the employer for his termination are a pretext for unlawful discrimination.

FAILURE TO FOLLOW RULES AND DISCIPLINARY PROCEDURES

Just as an employer expects its employees to follow rules and policies, employees have similar expectations about their employers. Although a failure to follow rules and policies may not, in and of itself, provide a basis for a discrimination claim, an employer's failure to follow its own rules could support an employee's contention that the offered reason for discipline or termination is a pretext or cover-up for discrimination.

For example, let's revisit employee Jones from the preceding hypothetical situation. Let us suppose that the employer had an employee handbook containing a progressive discipline policy, which simply recommended counseling, an oral warning, a written warning, and suspension before termination. Employee Jones, however, was summarily terminated for tardiness. The employer's failure to follow its own procedure, although only recommended and not mandatory, may lead to an assumption by outside persons that there was an ulterior, that is, unlawful, motive at work.

If an employee is led to believe that certain steps will be followed before discipline or termination is implemented but those steps are not followed, an appearance of unfair or arbitrary employer conduct results. The employer's failure to adhere to its own policies also creates a potential basis for a jury to find that the reason offered for the employee's termination is merely a pretext for age discrimination.

AGE-RELATED REMARKS

Employers must remember that there is no such thing as an off-the-record discussion with an employee. Anything an employer says can and will be used against the company before the EEOC or in a court of law. Moreover, an ever-increasing number of cases involve the use of secret recordings made by employees who either sensed they were on their way out or who otherwise made a habit of recording conversations with supervisors and co-workers. That fact is not surprising. What is surprising are the types of ill-advised, age-related comments supervisors make or are baited into making on such tape recordings.

Even seemingly innocent remarks or questions, such as asking an employee about his or her retirement plans, can be argued as an indication of age bias. Comments relating to the need for "new blood" or "fresh faces" in the workplace appear time and again in age discrimination cases, as does the perennial favorite "you can't teach an old dog new tricks." These phrases, or other phrases that reflect a stereotype that younger is better, simply have no place in management's workplace speech. Even if the age-protected employee laughs at an ageist joke or remark, that response will not prevent him from later testifying that not only was the joke offensive, but that he felt he had to laugh to protect his job.

What is more damaging, however, is that age-related jokes or disparaging comments are used to mischaracterize an employer's motivation for a challenged employment decision, especially when the person who made the comment was a decision-maker. Employers must remember that most age discrimination claims are based on circumstantial evidence of unlawful bias (see chapter 2), and almost anything that allegedly sheds light on an employer's motivation for a challenged decision will be considered by the EEOC or a court. As a result, even innocuous remarks may be considered as evidence of age discrimination under the right circumstances.

Many courts have recognized that age-related remarks made by persons not involved in making the challenged employment decision, or that are made by a decision-maker at a remote time or in a different context, are not evidence of age bias. Instead, they are meaningless "stray remarks." However, whether a given comment is a "stray remark" or is related closely enough to the employment decision to be evidence of discrimination is made on a case-by-case basis. Employers have no guarantee that a comment that is similar in content and circumstances to one that was excluded in one case will be excluded in another case. The best way for an employer to avoid unpleasant results of age-related remarks is to train management not to make them in the first place.

JUST WHEN YOU THINK YOU'RE SAFE ...

One final common problem to avoid is the misconception that an employer is immune to suit if it can show, for example, that it replaced a terminated protected-age employee with another person in the protected class. In race, national origin, and gender discrimination actions, a former employee who is relying on circumstantial evidence of discrimination must prove that he or she was replaced by someone outside the protected class. For example, a female must show that she was replaced by a male. This requirement is not the case with age discrimination claims, however.

In 1996 the United States Supreme Court ruled that employees can establish a claim of age discrimination even if they were replaced by someone who was also within the protected age group. The terminated employee can make this claim by showing that the replacement employee is significantly younger than the terminated employee. The explanation is straightforward: the ADEA prohibits discrimination because of a person's age, not because a person is age 40 or older. Therefore, the fact that one person in the protected class has lost out to another person in the protected class is irrelevant, so long as he has lost out *because of his age.* Consider the following example. An employee who is age 53 is terminated, ostensibly for performance reasons. Within two months the employer has hired a replacement employee who is age 43. Although the replacement employee also is within the protected class, the 10-year age difference is significant enough to support an age discrimination claim, at least initially.

This rule does not allow an employee to base a claim on thin evidence—for example, a claim based on the replacement of a 58-year-old by a 55-year-old. Instead, an age discrimination claim requires evidence that is sufficient to create an inference that an employment decision was based on unlawful age bias. Such an inference cannot be drawn from the replacement of one employee with another employee who is "insignificantly" younger. Because the ADEA prohibits discrimination on the basis of age and not class membership, the fact that a replacement is "substantially" younger than the terminated employee is a far more reliable indicator of age discrimination than is the fact that the employee was replaced by someone outside the protected class.

CHAPTER 7

THE CORRELATION BETWEEN AGE AND EMPLOYEE COSTS

THE ADEA'S UNIQUE FEATURES

The ADEA includes some features not found in other antidiscrimination statutes. To begin with, while the ADEA mirrors the prohibitions against discrimination found in Title VII and the Americans with Disabilities Act, the ADEA balances those prohibitions with several exceptions. Probably the most significant exception is one that allows employers to take actions adversely affecting older employees as long as the action is based on "reasonable factors other than age."

Also, Congress has recognized that the cost of employee benefits increases as employees age. For example, it has been estimated that on average it costs an employer an additional 15 percent to insure an older employee as compared with a younger counterpart. Worried that such accelerating costs would dissuade employers from hiring older persons, Congress drafted the ADEA to allow employers to consider the higher costs of older employees when crafting benefits packages.

As a result of unique features such as these, in limited circumstances it is not unlawful under the ADEA for an employer to make decisions that adversely affect older employees.

ECONOMIC CONSIDERATIONS

A variety of factors, such as higher salaries, greater benefits eligibility, and higher health care costs, can make older employees with relatively long job tenure more costly. For example, the wages of an older employee are often higher than those of a younger employee in the same job because of seniority. For an employer who produces a uniformly priced good or service, all other factors being equal, the per unit cost of production is likely to be higher if more senior employees are used to produce the good or service. A prudent employer would consider additional factors in analyzing productivity and economic efficiency, such as whether older employees are more efficient producers because of experience and better decision-making skills. From a simple economic standpoint, nevertheless, such a business may be made more profitable by employing younger persons.

Consequently, for purely economic reasons, employers sometimes terminate those employees who are more expensive in terms of salary and benefits, particularly in reduction-in-force situations. These employers are then often forced to defend their business decisions in age discrimination lawsuits. The employer is left with the practical burden of proving that the fact that older employees were terminated, perhaps even in disproportionately high numbers, was only indirectly and circumstantially related to their age.

THE ADEA'S PROHIBITIONS

For many years, the courts disagreed over whether an employee could use evidence that he or she was terminated because of a factor related to age, such as benefit or salary costs, as evidence of age discrimination. Many courts permitted employees to prove age discrimination claims by using evidence that age-correlated factors motivated the challenged decision. Other courts held that the ADEA permitted employers to make reasonable economic choices so long as those decisions were based on actual economic realities and not stereotypical biases about older employees.

The United States Supreme Court finally resolved the dispute in 1993. The Supreme Court recognized that the ADEA's fundamental purpose is to prevent employers from relying on stereotypes about the productivity and competence of older employees in making employment decisions. The Court, however, concluded that age-correlated factors, especially economic ones such as pension costs, are "analytically distinct" from age and, therefore, they can be relied on as a basis for an adverse employment decision without violating the ADEA. The Court then held that an employer's decision to terminate an employee on the basis of his pension cost, which was tied to his years of service with the company rather than his age, did not violate the ADEA's prohibition against intentional age discrimination. The Court did leave open the possibility that a pension-based decision could violate other federal laws, such as the Employee Retirement Income Security Act.

Generally, an employee-plaintiff now may prove an age discrimination claim by (1) direct evidence of intentional age bias, such as a statement by management that it intended to discharge its older employees; (2) circumstantial evidence of intentional age bias, such as evidence of replacement by a significantly younger person; (3) evidence that an employer intentionally used an age-correlated factor that was *directly* related to age, such as pension eligibility tied directly to an employee's age rather than years of service; or (4) evidence that an employer intentionally relied on an age-correlated factor as a proxy for age, such as when an employer terminates higher-salaried employees not to save money but in order to adversely affect older employees.

Those methods of proof all support a finding that an employee suffered disparate treatment—that is, the employer treated some people less favorably than others because of age (see chapter 2). Some courts recognize disparate impact theory under the ADEA, however, which complicates any analysis of age-correlated factors. In those courts, reliance on an age-correlated factor, such as salary level, for an employment decision will be held to violate the ADEA if it results in a disproportionate impact on employees age 40 and older and it cannot be justified by business necessity (see chapter 2).

THE EMPLOYER'S BURDEN

It should be emphasized that in all courts—even those that have rejected disparate impact analysis in ADEA cases—an employer will be required in varying degrees to defend any decision to rely on age-correlated criteria as a basis for employment decisions. An employer should be ready to answer questions such as

- What factors or events prompted the initial decision to take the challenged employment action;

- Why did the employer choose a particular approach or set of criteria;

- Whether salary reductions or other alternative cost-cutting measures were considered;

- Why any alternative cost-cutting measures were not used;

- Whether the employer considered productivity losses when calculating cost savings; and

- Whether the employer's cost savings analysis included an objective comparison of the individual employee's productivity to his or her salary.

Even though the ADEA places the ultimate burden of proving age discrimination on the employee, as a practical matter a jury is unlikely to find in favor of an employer that is unable to explain its decision-making process in terms that are business related, reasonable, and fair.

THE INTERPLAY BETWEEN THE ADEA AND OTHER LAWS

Finally, employers should remember that although an employment decision based on factors such as salary and benefit costs may not violate the ADEA, it may violate other laws. For example, the Employee Retirement Income Security Act prohibits employers from terminating employees for the purpose of interfering with their rights to receive benefits. This prohibition applies both to pension/retirement benefits and to health benefits. The clearest violations of this provision occur when an employer terminates an employee to prevent her from becoming vested in a retirement plan or from receiving health benefits for a known medical condition. In both cases, the employer is motivated by a desire to save money, but in both cases the employer's action is illegal. This interplay between federal employment laws must be kept in mind when an employer is considering employee benefits as a potential area of cost savings.

CHAPTER 8

SPECIAL HIRING AND MANAGEMENT ISSUES

In addition to the common problems and cost-related issues already addressed, some basic hiring and management issues merit separate, brief discussion. These issues involve job advertisements, applications and interviews, employee testing, management stereotyping, and job training.

HIRING ISSUES

In the hiring process, there are three areas in which the language used by an employer can result in liability for age discrimination: job advertisements, applications and interviews.

Advertisements

The EEOC has issued interpretive guidelines on job advertising and pre-employment inquiries under the ADEA. In its accompanying policy statement, the EEOC explains that although soliciting age information of applicants is not an express violation of the ADEA, the commission is concerned about advertisements that suggest or specify a preference for certain age groups of applicants. The EEOC has determined that such inquiries may reflect an employer's intent not to consider applicants' individual qualifications. As explained in chapter 1, one of the basic purposes of the ADEA is to prohibit stereotypical thinking about workers in the protected age group and to simultaneously require individualized assessments of their capabilities.

Under the ADEA, as interpreted by the EEOC and many courts, employers must therefore avoid not only explicit age-based limitations in job advertisements but also language that may be an implicit deterrent to older persons. Employers may have no intent to discriminate, but if they establish job qualifications that tend to favor or encourage younger persons and discourage older persons they may violate the ADEA.

The EEOC has identified several examples from actual advertisements that it considers to be in violation of the ADEA. Advertisements containing preferences for certain age groupings, such as "age 25 to 35," or terms such as "young," "college student," "recent college graduate," "boy," and "girl" deter older persons from applying for jobs for which they may be objectively qualified. The EEOC also has determined that using language from the opposite end of the age spectrum violates the ADEA. For example, phrases such as "age 40 to 50," "age over 65," "retired person," or "supplement your pension" may fall afoul of the law because they may discourage or deter other persons also within the protected age group, but outside the specified subgroup, from applying.

Advertisement language that courts have found to violate the ADEA includes descriptive phrases such as "recent college graduate," "those unable to continue college," "1–2 years out of college," "excellent first job," and "recent high school graduate." Courts have held that such phrases tend to discourage older persons from applying for jobs for which they otherwise are qualified and also indicate an employer's preference for younger persons as employees.

Examples of terms and references that have been held not to violate the ADEA include "young office group," "athletically inclined," "junior executive," and "junior secretary." These phrases were construed by courts as relating to the office environment or the type of job at issue rather than the age of applicants. However, an employer should remember that slight variations in advertising language and related circumstantial facts can result in different interpretations and judicial holdings.

Advertisements that contain maximum experience levels for preferred applicants are problematic. An advertisement stating that "0–5 years of experience is preferred" or that "applicants must have no more than two years experience" may discourage older individuals from applying. Experience limitations also could be seen as euphemisms for age bias. Nonetheless, some jobs are truly entry level in nature and objective overqualification is a lawful disqualifier for those jobs. Advertisements for entry-level jobs should state that they are just that, and also expressly state that age is not a consideration.

Using the phrase "state age" (when applying) in an advertisement is not necessarily a violation of the ADEA because it is an age-neutral reference. However, age-neutral requests will in fact be closely scrutinized to ensure that they are being made for a lawful purpose. The EEOC, in effect, requires employers to justify even neutral age-related requests. Most of the time no job-related reason will be sufficient to justify requests for an applicant's age in the EEOC's opinion.

One example of a job-related reason that would support requests for age information is if the information relates to a bona fide occupational qualification (discussed in chapter 2). However, whether an occupational qualification is "bona fide" is a problematic determination, at best, for employers. Both the EEOC and the courts hold that this exception will be "narrowly construed." Lawful age qualifications, or restrictions, arise most often in the public or quasi-public sectors for jobs involving the public safety, such as law enforcement and airline pilot jobs. States also may have laws for public jobs with maximum age hiring restrictions or maximum length of service retirement restrictions. Such state laws still must meet the standard for a valid bona fide occupational qualification exception to be legal under the ADEA.

Those agencies and courts that have examined job advertisements for ADEA compliance have analyzed them in their entirety and have looked at the actual effect, if any, of the advertisement on the employer's hiring practices. Evidence of unlawful advertisements may include the language of the challenged advertisement, an individual's explanation of whether and how the advertisement discouraged him or her from applying, and a comparison of the employer's applicant flow data with other similarly situated employers. Applicant flow data may be particularly instructive on the effects of job advertisements. If an employer has applicant flow data that matches up well with similarly situated employers, it is relatively unlikely that the challenged advertisement will be found to be discriminatory. By the same token, if an employer's applicant flow data by comparison shows that significantly fewer individuals age 40 and older responded to its advertisement or were actually hired for the advertised position, then an inference of discrimination may be drawn.

Employers can and should take affirmative steps to limit the chances that their advertisements will be challenged under the ADEA. Employers should scrutinize advertisement language for explicit and implicit age references and for terms that might discourage older persons from seeking employment; advertisements should include a separate statement encouraging individuals in the protected age group to apply.

Applications and Interviews

As with advertisements, the EEOC states that application requests for age information do not necessarily violate the ADEA. Nevertheless, in the event of a challenge such requests will be closely scrutinized because they may tend to deter older individuals from applying for a job or indicate a discriminatory purpose on the part of the employer. Obviously, it is better to avoid age-related requests and their attendant risks.

If an employer determines that a lawful reason exists to request applicants' ages, such as a bona fide occupational qualification, EEOC regulations require that specific antidiscrimination language be included on the application form. The sample statement provided in the regulations says, not surprisingly, "The Age Discrimination in Employment Act of 1967 prohibits discrimination on the basis of age with respect to individuals who are at least 40 years of age." Furthermore, under the regulations the term "employment application" is construed in its broadest sense and is understood to include all written inquiries about employment; formal applications for employment or promotion; written summaries of an applicant's background; and written inquiries by employees about terms, conditions, or privileges of employment.

Interview questioning can violate the ADEA in much the same way as job advertisements and applications. Again, in summary, while the law has no express prohibition against an interviewer asking for an applicant's date of birth or age, usually no good reason can be found for doing so. The question the employer should always consider is whether age is actually related to the successful performance of the job duties at issue. Employers must bear in mind that seldom will age be a bona fide occupational qualification.

Accordingly, an employer should avoid interview questions that directly address an applicant's age as well as any that could indirectly disclose actual or approximate age. Examples of actual interview questions that some courts have found to be indicative of employer age bias include the obvious and not so obvious:

- "How old are you?"

- "What is your date of birth?"

- "Are you 40 or over?"

- "Are you a member of the American Association of Retired Persons?"

- "Isn't it great about the senior citizen discounts at the mall?"

The following are some actual examples of less obvious age-related questions:

- "How old are your children?"

- "How old are your grandchildren?"

- "How long ago did you graduate from college?"

- "What is your favorite musical era?"

In summary, questioning an applicant about his or her age serves only to provide the rejected applicant with evidence for an age discrimination claim.

Employers can obtain age data needed for legitimate business purposes, such as governmental reporting, after making an offer of employment. Employers also can obtain age data for workflow analyses directly from applicants through the use of tear-off sheets from the application form. Employers must ensure that age information is obtained anonymously and that it is not seen by the individuals who will be conducting interviews or making hiring decisions.

A final note on handling rejection of applicants is warranted. Employers look for an applicant who is the right fit for a job in terms of skill sets, education, and experience. If an applicant has more than the desired level of qualifications for a particular job it is common to refer to the applicant as being "overqualified." This term, or label, however, may be understood by the rejected applicant as being a proxy for age. Careful consideration should be made before an applicant is told that he or she did not get the job because of overqualification. A better response is simply that another applicant was chosen and that the employer does not discuss its hiring decisions.

COGNITIVE ABILITY TESTING

Cognitive ability testing presents interesting issues for any employer that seeks to test the thinking ability of applicants or employees. The EEOC's regulations state that if an employment practice, including a cognitive test, is the basis for alleged different treatment, when "such practice has an adverse impact on individuals within the protected age group, it can only be justified as a business necessity." The regulations also state that tests that are given under a defense of "reasonable factors other than age" will be scrutinized under the standards in the EEOC's "Uniform Guidelines on Employee Selection Procedures."

At the outset, the legal effect of the EEOC's regulations on employee selection testing must be considered. The regulations specifically refer to potential liability under disparate impact theory. As explained in chapter 2, however, a question exists as to whether disparate impact theory is viable under the ADEA. If disparate impact theory is not judicially recognized under the ADEA, then the EEOC's position on selection procedures, insofar as it is based on that theory of liability, would have no application.

Although most of the sections in the EEOC's guidelines on employee selection procedures address disparate impact issues and validation of employee selection tests, one section does address disparate treatment liability. Under this section, a selection test may not be used to treat an applicant or employee differently. This situation would occur when not all applicants or employees are required to take the same selection test for employment, promotion, or other employment opportunity. In other words, employer liability could occur if significantly different or more rigorous tests were applied to a person or persons within a legally protected class or if their tests were evaluated using standards different from those applied to persons outside the protected class. In those instances, employer liability may arise even if the challenged test has been properly validated.

EEOC regulations and guidelines make it clear that similarly situated applicants and employees should take the same selection tests; that is, tests should be uniform in substance and uniformly administered, and examinations should be uniformly evaluated. For example, the EEOC suggests that an applicant or employee should be given a prior version of a selection test if that is the version that the other applicants or employees competing for the job took. If the employer can demonstrate that a more recent version of the test was required by business necessity, however, the administering of different tests could have a lawful basis.

A practical question employers should answer before testing applicants or employees is whether a cognitive ability test is both useful and advisable. For most jobs, experience or educational requirements serve as functional equivalents for cognitive ability tests. For example, an applicant with a degree in electrical engineering can be expected to have the necessary cognitive ability to perform an electrical engineering position. The same can be said in terms of experience requirements for jobs not requiring a formal degree. Therefore, selection testing may not provide useful information although it will cost an employer time and money and expose the company to some risk of legal challenge, no matter how slight.

The advisability of cognitive ability testing also must be balanced against its usefulness. In performing such tests, for example, it should be presumed that an employer will determine that some applicants or employees do not have the cognitive ability to perform a specific job or certain tasks related to a job. This area may be ripe for discrimination claims based on a variety of legally protected characteristics, including race, gender, age, and disability. If, for example, a cognitive ability test showed that an applicant or employee has diminished or impaired cognitive abilities, he or she may then be entitled to legal protection as a qualified individual with a disability, or the test results may lend credence to a claim that the individual has a record of disability or was perceived by the employer as being disabled. While this scenario may lead to a claim other than an age discrimination claim, it is not one any employer wants to invite.

If an employer decides to use cognitive ability testing, it must be prepared to show that the test is job related. Objective and demonstrable evidence should be available that the test clearly indicates which person's thinking ability or mental aptitude will better enable him or her to perform the job at issue or an essential aspect of that job.

AGEIST STEREOTYPING

As discussed in chapter 1, the ADEA is intended in large part to combat stereotypical thinking about the abilities of older persons in the workforce. The Secretary of Labor's report on age discrimination, which prompted enactment of the ADEA, stated that there is "persistent and widespread use of age limits in hiring that in a great many cases can be attributed only to arbitrary discrimination against older workers on the basis of age and regardless of ability." The ADEA's legislative history states in relevant part that "[s]cientific research ... indicates that chronological age alone is a poor indicator of ability to perform a job."

Consequently, the text of the ADEA states that the law's purpose is "to promote employment of older persons based on their ability rather than age [and] to prohibit arbitrary age discrimination in employment."

The United States Supreme Court has explained that Congress, in passing the ADEA, acted out of concern that "older workers were being deprived of employment on the basis of inaccurate and stigmatizing stereotypes."

Despite congressional intent to eradicate such stereotyping, it continues to be relied on in some unknown number of employment decisions. Certainly, applicants and employees commonly argue in court cases that the defendant-employer viewed them in terms of a stereotype rather than on an individualized basis. In litigation, this kind of argument can be a powerful weapon against employers. For these reasons, an additional note on stereotyping in hiring and management decisions is warranted.

Of course, many potential work-related stereotypes exist about older persons, but at some level they all involve the perception that people, as they get older, do not perform as well. Examples of commonly encountered employment stereotypes include the following:

- Older persons are inflexible;

- Older persons are less productive;

- Older persons are less energetic;

- Older persons are less adaptable;

- Older persons are not innovative, or are not innovative enough for "today's" business conditions;

- Older persons have obsolete technical skills or cannot keep up with current technology;

- Older persons are not suited for working collaboratively in a team environment, as is now required by many businesses;

- Older persons require higher salaries and have higher medical costs;

- Older persons are simply waiting to retire and will not be around as long as younger persons;

- Older age means diminished physical and mental capacity and poorer health in general or greater risk of incapacity caused by a health problem; and,

- Older persons do not have the same enthusiasm they once had.

Most assuredly, these stereotypes may involve attributes that accurately describe some employees—but of any age! Such characteristics have no direct, constant correlation with age and, therefore, the ADEA requires employers to make an individualized assessment of a person's qualifications and abilities. (See chapter 7 regarding the correlation between age and employee costs.)

When reviewing an adverse employment decision involving an applicant or employee age 40 or older, a human resource manager must consider whether a stereotype underlies the decision. To reveal a supervisor's motivation, especially when a decision is questioned, the human resource manager should ask the supervisor specific questions about the applicant's qualifications or the employee's performance. In the latter instance, the supervisor's answers should be compared with any recent written performance evaluations, even if made by someone else. The supervisor should also be questioned closely about the basis for dissatisfaction with the applicant's qualifications or the employee's performance. The human resource manager has to listen carefully to the stated reasons: if a supervisor cannot provide specific examples of job-related deficiencies, the chances are that the supervisor may be relying on generalizations rather than an individualized assessment of capabilities.

Practically speaking, a lack of specific examples of job-related deficiencies also will make a claim brought by an applicant or employee much more difficult to defend. Such a lack opens the door for a plaintiff to argue that the employment decision was driven by a stereotypical view of older persons' abilities.

TECHNOLOGY TRAINING

The Secretary of Labor's 1965 report on age discrimination in employment noted that older persons in the workforce are "disproportionately undereducated and immobile." The Secretary's reference was to both lack of formal education and inadequate job skills among older employees, and the report called for retraining older employees to meet technological changes in the workplace.

More than three decades later, concerns about the job preparedness of older employees is at least as great, if not more so, than in 1965. It may be a truism, but the current pace of change in the workplace and in business technology is so rapid that it has become a challenge for most employees to keep up. For example, a recent estimate found that approximately 75 percent of all jobs in the U.S. economy now involve some type of computer use. Keeping up with changes is especially difficult for employees who have been trained and who have many years of experience with a certain type of technology that suddenly becomes obsolete, which is a commonplace scenario with computer-related technology. The challenge for the human resource professional is to keep older employees in the technology loop, so to speak, through uniformly applied, competent job training.

Some older employees, it is true, have not kept pace with technological changes in their industries and, as a result, they have become less valuable to their employers. However, it would be stereotypical ageism to think that older employees generally fall into such a category. Older employees not only keep current with job-related technology, but many are in jobs for which their prior experience, for example with earlier versions of software, can be invaluable to younger coworkers and the employer.

Human resource professionals have several commonsensical ways to assist older employees with technology-related job training. First, the human resource professional has to make all employees understand that the increasingly technical nature of their jobs, that is, the growth of computer-related technology with all its benefits and all its faults, is here to stay. At the same time all employees should clearly understand that they will have to know how to competently use job-related technology in order to remain employed. In other words, employees should be put on notice that competent use of related technology is an essential function of an increasing number of jobs.

Second, employees should receive training on all technology they will be asked to use. This may seem like an obvious statement, but too often employees are simply put to work on a computer without any training or without enough training. Job training, of course, can come in a variety of forms; the only requirement is that it adequately cover the topic and be uniformly available to all employees. This latter point may require an employer to offer flexible training modes to ensure that all employees have the same opportunity for training. For example, some employees will need flexible training schedules for work-related or personal, such as child care, reasons.

After training is conducted, a supervisor or human resource professional should check with employees about their training. An employee should be given the chance to ask follow-up questions, and this encounter also gives an employer the opportunity to assess the effectiveness of training. Finally, it is imperative both for internal business uses and any subsequent related litigation that adequate records of all job training be maintained.

One way to encourage and, in fact, mandate that all employees participate in training at the desired level is to require regular technology "certification" classes. Such certifications also could be required before an employee is permitted to use a given technology. If a technology certification is required, an employee's ability or inability to achieve certification can be used as an objective method to determine whether an employee can perform the job adequately. If competent use of job-related technology is truly an essential function of a job, then an employee's inability to achieve certification should be a lawful basis for discipline or termination.

The importance of adequate job training cannot be overemphasized. Not only is it valuable to the company as a whole, but it also serves to defeat one of the most frequent refrains by plaintiffs in employment discrimination cases, which is the "I didn't get the training I needed" comment. This allegation is repeated virtually every time an employee is terminated for performance. Plaintiffs, rather than critically examining their own performance, find it far easier to point the finger at their former employer and allege that it did not give them the necessary tools for success. The employer, for its own sake, better be able to prove the aggrieved employee wrong.

CHAPTER 9

ADVICE TO COMPANIES SUED BY THEIR EMPLOYEES: DON'T TAKE IT PERSONALLY

Editor's Note: This chapter was authored by Ross P. Laguzza, Ph.D., of DecisionQuest, Inc.

No corporation enjoys being sued, yet most accept litigation as a cost of doing business. Most cases, even the very large cases, tend to be managed in a businesslike fashion. In other words, while the corporation may make a high intellectual and financial investment in the litigation management, little emotion is involved. The level and type of involvement often change, however, when the plaintiff is a current or former employee. Often the plaintiff targets key individuals along with the company and alleges some manner of unfair treatment on the job. Something about being called unfair in this context raises the hackles of many a defendant, particularly those who are convinced that they did nothing wrong and that the suit is completely unjustified and frivolous. This situation often leads to a high level of emotional investment in the case, which in turn can lead to trouble at trial.

THE IRRESISTIBLE URGE TO ATTACK THE PLAINTIFF: IT'S A MATTER OF PRINCIPLE

Once people at the company become emotionally involved in a case, their judgment about how to prepare for trial becomes impaired. This impairment is typically manifested as a desire to prove to the jury that the plaintiff is an undeserving and wretched human being who has fabricated a tale of woe to cover his or her own inadequacies and failings. Defending the case becomes a matter of principle and exposing the plaintiff's avarice. "We won't give that *%@% one dollar!" is a familiar battle cry heard during trial preparation discussions. The basic trial strategy is to attack the plaintiff, expose any deficiencies, and thus destroy any trace of sympathetic connection between jury and plaintiff. This strategy is an emotionally gratifying one. Dehumanizing the plaintiff feels good. Attacking the plaintiff feels good. Nothing is quite so psychologically exquisite as anticipating squashing the enemy. The only problem is that this strategy usually fails and losing big feels really bad.

Frequently, outside counsel, in an attempt to support their client and satisfy their objectives, become intoxicated by their client's emotional involvement in the case. They then quickly and unfortunately take up the battle cry "kill the plaintiff!" and place objectivity not in the back seat, but in the trunk where it is then wrapped tightly in a lead blanket. Case preparation becomes a contest to see who can display the least impulse control. Key company witnesses, if not specifically trained to kill, certainly pick up on the "blood in the water" spirit of the trial team and incorporate attacking messages into their testimony and nonverbal behavior. The result is a well-oiled killing machine that is revved up and headed for a precipice that would make Thelma and Louise proud.

WHY ATTACKING THE PLAINTIFF MAY BE HAZARDOUS TO YOUR HEALTH

If you haven't figured this out already, the thesis I am arguing here is that in most employment cases, blaming and attacking the plaintiff is not only a bad idea, but also it can so inflame the jury members that they are motivated to teach the company a very personal lesson on how employees should be treated. It is important to pause here for a moment and underscore that attacking the plaintiff as a strategy fails even with truly undeserving employees. Why? Years of empirical research on this question kept leading to a single, albeit broad, construct that seemed to explain all relevant juror behavior in employment trials. Careful study of the elements encompassed by this construct indicates that when you strip everything else away, what jurors in employment cases really care about is "safety." This label was selected as one that best summarizes the types of things jurors perceive, believe, and argue in employment litigation. In fact, it now appears that concerns about safety form the core of juror experience in these types of cases and is a recurring theme in hundreds of interviews with real and surrogate jurors. These interviews show that for a typical juror, nothing is more threatening than the prospect of an unsafe workplace.

Most jurors easily identify with an unsafe workplace either because they believe they have experienced one firsthand, or because *they are afraid they might experience one sometime in the future.* For the reader who imagines that the safety construct applies only to jobs involving risk to life and limb, please read on. Threats to safety encompass more than just threats to physical safety and include unfair or inconsistent recognition and reward, verbal harassment, unwillingness to listen, unwillingness to change, lack of nurturing, lack of proper training and counseling, inconsistent consequences, inadequate warnings, and countless others. So this construct refers to one's psychological safety as well as safety from physical harm. Since most people derive a tremendous amount of psychological value from their jobs (i.e., self-esteem), it is no surprise to learn that people serving on juries evaluate the quality of a work environment by examining how well it allows people to satisfy these less tangible but highly important needs. A workplace that interferes or undermines this important function is seen as less safe than one that proactively supports and protects it.

People who serve on employment juries tend to have very high, if not unrealistic, expectations about employers' responsibilities for providing a safe work environment. Using hindsight, jurors always believe the company could have done more to protect an employee from a bad experience and its attendant stress (i.e., more training, more warnings, more counseling, more accommodation). The situation is not that people serving on juries don't understand the court case, as many lawyers and lay people suspect. Nor are they living in a fantasy world in which employees are held blameless for their transgressions. Instead, jurors tend to define their task much more broadly than evaluating the specifics of a particular dispute. These men and women often see their role as one of safeguarding the world of work for themselves and everyone else. This mission, distorted as it may be, serves as a powerful filter through which case information is processed and formed into a final verdict. This mission may have been best articulated by a juror who, when asked about whether his expectations for employee treatment were realistic, said: "I know it is not the way it really is, but our verdict reflects the way we think it should be."

Corporate clients often do not adequately consider these safety factors in evaluating their cases, or they discount the importance of the factors because they can be "reasonably explained." They don't fully appreciate that, from the jurors' perspective, the road to a safe workplace is quite narrow indeed and even small deviations are seen as treacherous.

It also is critical to understand that concerns about workplace safety are automatically activated in any type of employment litigation. Jurors assume that if an employee is suing, something must have been unsafe about the workplace. Jurors tend to look past the plaintiff's deficiencies and focus on the quality and quantity of the threats present on the job. Almost always, a jury verdict in an employment case can be understood as a desire to minimize or eliminate a real or perceived threat in the workplace, not just for the plaintiff, *but for all employees, everywhere.* In this regard, jurors as human beings who currently work or who are close to those who do are motivated to make the world of work as safe as possible. It is easy to appreciate how jurors, so motivated, could perceive an attack on the plaintiff, no matter how meritorious, as directly counter to their expectations of an employer committed to an employee's welfare. Combined with other anti-company biases individual jurors might harbor, such attacks tend to stir up a rather toxic stew.

THE CASE OF THE GENTLE GIANT

A case involving a male employee who claimed he was sexually harassed by a female supervisor provides an excellent example of the problems associated with attacking a plaintiff in employment litigation. The plaintiff was a 28-year-old male, a former marine who at 6 feet 3 inches and 250 pounds towered over his 5-foot-1-inch, 100-pound female supervisor. In his petition he alleged that his supervisor would regularly sexually harass and humiliate him during work by, among other things, jumping onto his lap, straddling him, and simulating sexual intercourse. He said he was helpless to fend off these unwanted advances and feared that if he reported them to anyone, she would retaliate against him. Ultimately, some other employee reported the conduct, it was investigated, and this lawsuit was born. In early trial strategy sessions, the corporate client and his attorney were nearly salivating at the chance of putting this scenario in front of the jury. In their minds, the jury would never believe that this hulk of a man, who at one time had hundreds of soldiers under his command, would allow anyone, certainly not this woman, to do anything he did not want him or her to do. Their expressed goals at the time were "to prove to the jury that this guy is lying" and "to really nail this guy in front of the jury." In short, it was a team in full attack mode.

Fortunately, the plaintiff's deposition had been videotaped and was incorporated into a pretrial research study, which gave us a chance to study how jurors would likely process this plaintiff's story. In his deposition, the plaintiff was soft spoken, unassertive, and shy. He indicated he had attended a college that was known to jurors in the venue to provide a strict religious education. Many jurors interpreted this fact to mean he probably was much more sensitive to any form of sexual conduct and perhaps was ill equipped to know how to deal with this behavior. After watching him testify for some time, the jurors came to believe he was sincere and not just putting on an act. After that point, they began to describe him as the "gentle giant." They believed he was the type of person who, despite his enormous size, was powerless when it came to dealing with certain matters, especially those involving confrontations with the opposite sex. His testimony about how he "just sat there," motionless, while his supervisor allegedly bounced around in his lap, was all quite believable once jurors constructed the gentle giant profile. The jurors, especially female jurors, became quite protective of the plaintiff and strongly resented any attacks on his character, behavior, or motivation by the defendant. Even some of the most "macho" male jurors were willing to reconsider the case in light of the gentle giant phenomenon constructed by their fellow jurors.

Whether the presumptions about the "gentle giant" were all true or not did not matter, because jurors believed them to be true. In short, the defense plan backfired and jurors wanted to take action that would ensure the company got the message about how all employees deserve protection from harassment on the job. Needless to say, the client was not happy with this latest wrinkle in its plans.

PLAYING THE SAFETY GAME TO WIN

Spirits seemed to improve somewhat once we encouraged the trial team to give up on their objective "to get this guy" and instead focus on an issue jurors were more likely to care about. The secret to building a persuasive defense story in employment litigation is to *identify how the plaintiff's case threatens workplace safety*. This objective is always more easily said than done, is different for every case, and often requires much creative problem solving and message testing. Yet, developing this theme has proven time and again to be the best way to motivate jurors to think critically about the plaintiff's claims *and* (ironically) to encourage them to focus on any of the plaintiff's shortcomings.

In the case of the gentle giant, we recommended a strategy that downplayed the question, as tempting as it was, of why he did not put a stop to any unwanted behavior and focused on the question of why he did not *report* the behavior to anyone else. The company did have a number of accessible and anonymous reporting methods in place and a reasonably vigorous enforcement policy. Our goal was to show that while the plaintiff may have felt helpless and intimidated by the supervisor while the behavior was occurring, he was not so helpless that he could not avail himself of the company's anonymous reporting phone line when he was away from the situation. After all, the alleged conduct took place out in the open and any number of other employees could have made the report (and, in fact, one ultimately did). While this part of the message was important, what really made it salient to jurors is that by choosing not to take any steps to report this inappropriate behavior, he put other employees at risk for the same type of treatment. The plaintiff, in a sense, was essentially claiming to have no ability and no responsibility for protecting himself or others, which if true is a belief that threatens everyone's safety. If no individual feels responsible for making the workplace safe, then all individuals are at risk. The defendants also argued that by not giving the company's anti-harassment policies and procedures a chance to work, the plaintiff actually exacerbated and prolonged his difficulties with this supervisor.

When this theory was tested in a research setting, jurors were much more likely to criticize the plaintiff's failure to report and much less critical of the company. They naturally remained concerned about the supervisor's behavior but were less inclined to blame the company for the fact that it took place. The key advantage of the new strategy was that it no longer required jurors to find the plaintiff undeserving as a person in order to give some consideration to the defense position. They could still sympathize with the gentle giant, while at the same time hold him responsible for not doing the minimum to protect himself and his fellow employees. The tone of the defense was not to convey that the company believed he was a bad person, but that his choices in handling the matter interfered with the company's ability to help him (i.e., to make his workplace safer for him). This story was much easier for the defense to tell and positioned the company as concerned about employee safety and not antagonistic toward one of its own employees.

THE CASE OF THE HEARTLESS UTILITY

Now we will turn to the case of the utility that laid off hundreds of employees, many of whom happened to be over 40 years of age. A subset of this group filed suit alleging age discrimination. The company's first inclination was to attack these plaintiffs as greedy malcontents who did not deserve to live (or something to that effect) and then to defend the rationale for the layoffs. Again, pretrial research indicated that this strategy was ineffective and created significant agitation among the jurors. In the research exercise, jurors were convinced this company did not care about long-term employees who had dedicated their lives to the company. The jurors were angry and wanted to make the company suffer for placing profits over people. The more the company defended its conduct, the angrier and more punitive jurors became.

Again, we went back to the drawing board and carefully thought about what these jurors were trying to teach us. We discovered that one issue they really cared about was that the company always placed the best person in the job, no matter what his or her age. This discovery led us to propose a "retracted claw" approach, which was based on the core idea that a company has the right and the obligation to always select the best person for the job. We knew from the previous research that jurors were more likely to identify with a message that reflected one of their core values; that is, a safe workplace is one in which merit takes precedence over demographics. By making this message the core theme of the defense case and adding messages about how the plaintiffs did have control over the selection process, the trial team was able to neutralize the natural sympathy engendered by the plaintiffs and give jurors a reason to feel good about voting for the company. It was also obvious to jurors how the plaintiffs' case threatened the concept of a safe workplace. If merit was less important than someone's age for example, many qualified people would be at a significant disadvantage. This theme played to younger and older jurors alike and ultimately persuaded the real jury at trial, which resulted in a resounding defense verdict.

IT'S NOT FAIR

Sometimes, employment litigation plaintiffs are less than deserving people. Sometimes, when a current or former employee says he or she was they were treated unfairly on the job, key witnesses and others at the company feel they have been personally attacked. The natural reaction in these situations is to fight fire with fire. Repeated experiences and careful study of how jurors think about these cases suggest an alternative approach, which frankly is not nearly as cathartic but is far more likely to produce an outcome with which the company can live. As you may have surmised, the focus on the safety construct not only pays dividends during trial, but it also offers many lessons for how workplace policies and procedures should be managed to minimize the risk of litigation in the first place.

In the throes of battle, people at the company may say "but this guy is a jerk, it is not fair if he is allowed to come to trial and pretend otherwise." While this statement may be true, it should not be mistaken for a viable trial strategy. In the end, even the most emotionally involved client would agree that the court case is not really about attacking the plaintiff, it is about facilitating the jury's identification with the defense and thereby increasing the chances of a defense verdict. Put another way, it is much easier to deal with some pent-up emotional frustration than a multimillion-dollar plaintiff verdict.

CHAPTER 10

THE ADMINISTRATIVE PROCESS

When the ADEA was enacted in 1967 the administrative agency responsible for its enforcement was the United States Department of Labor. In the 1978 amendments to the ADEA, administrative responsibility was given to the EEOC to complement its oversight of the other major antidiscrimination statute at the time, Title VII of the Civil Rights Act of 1964. The administrative process for charges that allege ADEA violations is similar to the administrative process for Title VII claims but is different in some important ways.

FILING A CHARGE OF DISCRIMINATION

To be timely, a charge alleging a violation of the ADEA must be filed with the EEOC within 180 days of the alleged discriminatory act, unless the alleged discrimination occurs in a state that has its own age discrimination laws and an administrative agency responsible for their enforcement. In that event, the charge must be filed with the EEOC within 300 days of the alleged unlawful act, or 30 days after receipt of the notice that the state agency has completed its investigation of the charge, whichever occurs earlier. Virtually all states now have laws against age discrimination in employment and they have agencies to enforce those laws. As a result, the 300-day filing rule applies almost universally. The timeliness issue, however, can be technical. Therefore, any time a charge is filed more than 180 days after the alleged discriminatory act it would be wise to carefully consider whether a timeliness issue is present. This chapter addresses only federal administrative filing requirements.

In the event a person believes that he or she has been discriminated against because of age, the process for redress starts with the filing of a timely EEOC charge. In addition to basic information about the employee (the "charging party" or "claimant") and the employer (the "charged party" or "respondent"), an EEOC charge must provide a clear and concise statement of the facts, including relevant dates, constituting the alleged unlawful employment practice.

Upon receipt of the charge, the EEOC is required to notify the respondent within 10 days that a charge has been filed against it. A copy of the charge, a detailed request for information from the respondent, and a request for the respondent's statement of facts usually accompany the notice of the charge.

The ADEA and the EEOC's regulations provide that a charging party cannot bring legal action against the respondent until at least 60 days after the charge is filed with the EEOC. The waiting period, also called the "conciliation period," is intended to give the EEOC an opportunity to conciliate, or resolve, the dispute. During the 60-day conciliation period the EEOC will attempt to investigate the charge. It is not unusual for the investigation process to extend well beyond 60 days, but a charging party may file suit any time after the expiration of 60 days. In that event, the EEOC will terminate its investigation of the charge.

RESPONDING TO A CHARGE OF DISCRIMINATION

After receiving a charge and notifying the respondent, the EEOC will require the respondent to provide a "position statement" addressing the allegations made by the party who is charging discrimination. It also will require that the respondent provide responses to several detailed information requests that the EEOC considers necessary for its investigation and conciliation efforts. In addition to seeking the respondent's side of the story, the EEOC typically will ask a number of questions about the respondent's business, such as whether it has government contracts, the names and addresses of other employees with similar employment circumstances as the charging party, and other general questions. Often these requests are extremely broad, difficult to understand, and not apparently relevant to any claim made by the charging party.

Responses to EEOC Requests

In responding to the EEOC's request for information, the employer's goal, frankly, is not to satisfy the EEOC by providing all the information it requests. An employer must remember that the EEOC investigatory process often is a preliminary step in what could be a lengthy process of federal court litigation. Although a prudent respondent should not go out of its way to antagonize the EEOC and it should be reasonably cooperative and timely, an accession to all the EEOC's demands will not ensure a successful resolution of the dispute.

Unless the EEOC can effect a settlement, two outcomes to the administrative process typically occur: (1) the EEOC finds no reasonable basis for the charging party's claim (a "no cause" determination); or (2) the EEOC finds that there is reason to believe that the ADEA has been violated by the respondent. Although the former outcome is much preferred to the latter, the end result usually is the same—the EEOC issues a "notice of right to sue" to the charging party, which entitles him or her to pursue legal action within 90 days of its receipt, usually in federal court.

A "no cause" determination by the EEOC does not preclude legal action. Indeed, the EEOC's determination has little or no impact on the judicial proceedings that routinely follow. Accordingly, although a "no cause" determination is initially satisfying, it is not really a "win" in a substantive sense and it will not protect against suit. Indeed, elaborate responses to the EEOC's information requests in the hope that a "no cause" determination will be issued only provide a potential plaintiff with much information early in the case that will assist his or her attorney in crafting a case against the employer. Any "win" at the EEOC level, therefore, loses its luster if information was given to the EEOC that then will be used against the respondent in a related lawsuit.

Furthermore, after the EEOC concludes an investigation, information provided to it is subject to disclosure under the federal Freedom of Information Act. Accordingly, employers should understand that information provided to the EEOC may end up as "Plaintiff's Exhibit 1" in a related civil action. Likewise, information provided by the charging party is subject to disclosure and should be obtained. Often the charging party's initial story to the EEOC is different from the story advanced after suit is filed. Such discrepancies can be very helpful in defending claims.

In responding to the EEOC's information request, an initial determination of relevance to the charging party's claim should be made and only reasonably relevant information should be provided. For example, the information provided to the EEOC should be restricted to a reasonable time frame in relation to the date of the alleged discriminatory act and to a reasonable geographic area as determined by the charging party's place of employment. Simply because the EEOC has requested information does not mean that it must be provided. Often the EEOC's information requests are "boilerplate" in nature, and little attention has been given to tailoring the requests to the facts of the charging party's situation.

If the respondent concludes that an information request is overly broad, then we do not recommend that the EEOC be asked to limit the scope of its information requests. Rather, the best approach is for the respondent to unilaterally provide what it considers to be appropriate. If the EEOC then determines that it needs more information, it is free to request it. The request for additional information should then be evaluated by the respondent as to relevance and reasonableness.

Administrative Subpoenas

If the respondent and the EEOC disagree about the scope of the information to be provided, the EEOC has the authority to issue an administrative subpoena in an attempt to coerce the respondent to provide additional information. It is important to remember that an administrative subpoena is not the equivalent of a judicial subpoena. If a judicial subpoena is disregarded, then the subpoenaed party will be subject to contempt of court proceedings. An EEOC subpoena does not initially carry that threat of penalty. The EEOC has no authority to enforce its subpoenas or to issue fines to a noncompliant respondent.

If an administrative subpoena is received from the EEOC that the respondent believes is unreasonable for any reason, the respondent—through its counsel—should write the EEOC office that issued the subpoena and explain its objections and what, if anything, will be provided. The parties may be able to work out the disagreement at that level. If not, and the respondent ultimately refuses to accede to the EEOC's demands, then the EEOC must seek enforcement from the local federal court.

Before that step is taken by the EEOC, the file first is submitted to the regional federal Solicitor's office. This usually will mark the first involvement by an attorney on behalf of the EEOC. A reasonable resolution often can be negotiated with the Solicitor's representative. However, if enforcement proceedings are initiated and the federal court orders that the requested information be provided, failure to do so will then subject the respondent to a citation for contempt of court, as well as potential fines and imprisonment.

In short, a respondent is not obliged to provide the EEOC with anything unless a court orders the respondent to do so. Prudence, however, warrants a reasonable response to the EEOC's information requests and administrative subpoenas. A wise respondent will limit its responses to a reasonable time frame, a relevant geographical area, and information that is plainly relevant to the charging party's allegations.

The respondent should take great care to provide accurate information in whatever responses it gives. Any admissions against an employer's interests or misstatements of facts, including inadvertent ones, made in an EEOC response can and undoubtedly will be used as evidence against the respondent at trial. Accordingly, responses to any requests for information by the EEOC should not be made haphazardly. Also, before any information is provided, an investigation of the allegations should be made to minimize the chance that EEOC responses are inconsistent with a defense that will be presented in court.

In short, EEOC responses should be viewed as the opening event in a series of events that may end in a federal trial. If theories and facts placed before the EEOC are inconsistent with theories and facts put forward at trial, an employer can be sure that the inconsistencies will be highlighted by the plaintiff's counsel, often with the assertion that the respondent tried to mislead the United States government.

THE EEOC'S ROLE IN THE ADMINISTRATIVE PROCESS

The EEOC is not the respondent's friend; it is charged with enforcing the nation's federal antidiscrimination laws. At the administrative level, those laws are liberally construed in favor of the charging party. Although the EEOC should not be treated, or viewed, as the enemy, the respondent should remember that it is involved in an adversarial process whenever it is dealing with the EEOC.

Often a charging party views the EEOC as merely a statutorily required step on his or her way to the federal courthouse. Many charging parties and their lawyers do not really expect the EEOC to provide them with a substantive benefit; nevertheless, a charge must be filed before the charging party is able to file suit. A respondent should keep this reality in mind when confronted with an EEOC charge and the accompanying information requests.

THE ROLE OF OUTSIDE COUNSEL

Although legal counsel is not required to navigate the administrative process, a respondent should seriously consider obtaining outside counsel knowledgeable in civil rights issues at the first step of the process. Competent counsel can assist in formulating responses that conform with the law but cause no harm in subsequent related litigation. Outside counsel also will be involved at the "ground floor" when defenses and positions are being formulated. The early formulation of a consistent story and defense is of critical importance.

Depending on the complexity of the potential case, knowledgeable outside counsel should be content to let the respondent draft responses, which counsel then reviews and revises if necessary. This type of early involvement of outside counsel is cost effective and could result in substantial overall savings if the case develops into a lawsuit. As a part of this strategy, serious consideration should be given to using the counsel's letterhead rather than the respondent's for making EEOC responses; this step minimizes the legal effect of having misstatements of fact be directly attributed to the respondent. Although it might seem a small matter, it is much easier to explain away a discrepancy advanced in a letter from counsel as opposed to a letter on the respondent's letterhead.

This recommendation is not to suggest that outside counsel should be used to advance positions not supported by fact and law. Rather, counsel can be used to insulate the respondent from inadvertent admissions and inaccurate factual positions before the EEOC. As a case moves through the litigation process, facts often come to light that were not known earlier and defenses often change as a case develops. If outside counsel is initially used to forward information to the EEOC, the respondent has greater flexibility in responding to developing facts.

Great care should be given when formulating EEOC responses. The responses given to the EEOC can and probably will be used against the respondent at trial if the responses are at odds with the fully developed facts or are different from a trial defense.

CHAPTER 11

REMEDIES

Court-ordered relief for employment discrimination has two purposes; first, it is intended to "make whole" the victim of unlawful employment discrimination, and, second, it is intended to serve the broader social goals of remedying past discrimination and preventing future discrimination by employers. Under the "make whole" standard, courts may not order or award relief that would put victims of unlawful discrimination in a better position than they would have been in otherwise. For example, victimized employees may recover actual lost wages but not excess wages, or they may be reinstated to the same or a comparable job but not a better job.

The types of remedies generally available under the federal anti-discrimination statutes include injunctive relief, such as a court order that an employer take or refrain from taking some action; equitable relief, such as an award of money for lost wages; and legal damages, such as an award of money for emotional distress or to punish an exceptionally bad act of discrimination.

REMEDIES UNDER THE ADEA

The type of remedies and amount of relief that may be recovered under the ADEA are limited in comparison to the remedies available under other federal antidiscrimination laws and some state fair employment laws. For example, legal damages for emotional distress and punitive damages (in a combined amount up to $300,000, depending on the size of the employer) are available under Title VII and the Americans with Disabilities Act. Many states also allow recovery of emotional distress and punitive damages—in unlimited amounts—under wrongful termination claims.

Under the ADEA, in contrast, a successful plaintiff may not recover emotional distress or punitive damages. Instead, only four types
of equitable relief are potentially available: (1) compensation for lost
wages ("back pay"); (2) reinstatement or instatement (i.e., an order to
hire) of employment; (3) compensation for future wages ("front pay"),
but only if reinstatement is not possible; and (4) "liquidated damages."
Injunctive relief also is available under the ADEA, and the costs of
litigation and attorneys fees also may be awarded to a successful
plaintiff's lawyer (although fees are rarely, if ever, awarded to successful defense counsel).

The explanation for the difference in remedies between the ADEA
and other antidiscrimination laws is found in chapter 1. In short, age
discrimination has a different social history than other kinds of prohibited discrimination. For example, the origins of other kinds of discrimination, such as racial discrimination, are found outside the employment sphere and, thus, they are considered more socially
destructive than age discrimination, which usually stems solely from
the employment relationship. Furthermore, at least a loose correlation
sometimes exists between age and lawful employment considerations,
such as performance capabilities and costs. As a result, Congress has
made a policy-based decision that age discrimination is less deleterious
than other types of prohibited discrimination and has accordingly limited the remedies available to victims of age discrimination.

Following is a brief description of the types of relief available
under the ADEA.

Back Pay

Back pay is the initial monetary relief granted to individuals who
are subject to age discrimination. It is most commonly awarded in termination cases, but it also can be awarded in failure-to-hire and promotion cases. Back pay compensates an employee for wages lost as a
result of the employer's discriminatory act.

The amount of back pay that can be recovered by a successful
ADEA plaintiff is the amount of wages the employee would have

earned between the date of the discriminatory act, that is, the date of termination or failure to hire or promote, and the date of the judgment in his or her favor. This calculation includes not only lost wages, but also the dollar value of other benefits of employment such as insurance, profit sharing, and vacation pay. Any interim earnings the employee has received during this time period are then subtracted from this amount to determine the back pay award.

The back pay award will be further reduced to the extent that an employee fails to satisfy his or her duty to mitigate, or reduce, damages. An ADEA claimant is required to make diligent efforts to obtain suitable alternative employment between the date of termination and trial. If a plaintiff obtains comparable employment or fails to make reasonable efforts to do so, the accrual of back pay damages will be cut off.

A number of other events may terminate the accrual of back pay. One of these events is a bona fide, unconditional offer of reinstatement by the former employer of the same or a comparable position with the same rate of pay and benefits. "Unconditional" means that the former employee must not be required to dismiss or release the right to file a lawsuit as a condition of reinstatement. In some jurisdictions, back pay also can be reduced by sources of collateral income such as severance pay, social security benefits, disability payments, or pension benefits.

Front Pay

In most jurisdictions, an ADEA plaintiff also may be entitled to an award of front pay. Front pay is compensation for future economic losses, that is, wage and benefit loss, that results from an act of age discrimination and that cannot be remedied by reinstatement, hiring, or promotion. Entitlement to front pay is a matter to be determined by the court, not a jury. Front pay will not be awarded when reinstatement (discussed below) of an employee is ordered by the court. Also, if the court determines that the plaintiff has mitigated his or her damages by finding suitable new employment or, alternatively, has failed to mitigate damages when he or she could have, front pay will not be awarded. In other words, front pay may be appropriate when a former employee has made suitable efforts to find alternative employment but has been unable to do so through no fault of his or her own. Front pay entitlement also can be cut off in the same manner as back pay, for example, by an unconditional offer of reinstatement.

If a former employee is entitled to front pay, the amount is based on evidence of how long it will take the former employee to obtain similar employment under local economic conditions. For example, if the court determines that a claimant should be able to obtain comparable employment within two years from the date of trial, the court will award front pay in the amount of two years of salary and benefits, less any amounts actually earned or that could have been earned from mitigation efforts. This figure then is reduced to its "present value" to avoid a windfall to the plaintiff. As with back pay, the amount of front pay can sometimes be reduced by collateral sources of income.

Reinstatement

The ADEA enables courts to fashion and award relief as is appropriate to further the purposes of the act. Accordingly, a court can require an employer to reinstate (or hire or promote) a successful ADEA plaintiff. Reinstatement is the preferred remedy under the ADEA because the purpose of the ADEA, like that of all antidiscrimination laws, is to get and keep protected persons in the active workforce, not to provide them a monetary windfall. This remedy is in keeping with the "make whole" nature of employment discrimination remedies generally. Therefore, courts can and usually will order reinstatement even if the successful former employee prefers a monetary award. However, reinstatement obviously is not mandatory. As noted, an award of front pay can be awarded when reinstatement is not practical. Reinstatement is impractical when the degree of hostility between the former employer and employee makes a productive employment relationship unlikely.

Liquidated Damages

A successful ADEA plaintiff also may be entitled to an award of liquidated damages if it is proven that the employer's violation of the ADEA was "willful." The purpose of liquidated damages is to compensate a victim of age discrimination for damages too obscure and difficult to prove and also to act as a deterrent to future violations of the act. In certain respects, liquidated damages are similar to awards of punitive damages under other statutes. What type of conduct constitutes a "willful" violation is somewhat vague. Generally, an employer acts "willfully" either when it knew its conduct violated the ADEA or it acted in reckless disregard of whether its conduct was unlawful. An employer does not act willfully if it had a good faith belief that it was not violating the ADEA, or if it simply acted negligently. Whether particular acts constitute a willful violation is determined on a case-by-case basis.

If liquidated damages are awarded, the amount is limited to a doubling of the award of back pay. For example, if a former employee is awarded $10,000 in back pay, liquidated damages would be limited to another $10,000 award. If no back pay is awarded, no award of liquidated damages is possible.

Emotional Distress and Punitive Damages

The great majority of courts have held that emotional distress damages, that is, pain and suffering, and punitive damages may not be recovered under the ADEA. However, a few courts have held to the contrary. Also, as noted below, an ADEA claimant may attempt to circumvent this prohibition by bringing state law claims that allow for the recovery of emotional distress and punitive damages.

Costs And Attorney Fees

The ADEA authorizes an award of costs and attorney fees to a prevailing plaintiff. Although some jurisdictions have held that it is within the jurisdiction of the court to determine whether fees should be awarded, most courts will award fees to a successful ADEA claimant as a matter of course. All courts, however, will exercise discretion in determining the amount of costs and fees to be awarded. A prevailing employer in an ADEA lawsuit will not be entitled to its attorney fees unless it can prove that the lawsuit was frivolous and brought in bad faith. This burden is an extremely high one for an employer to sustain. In all likelihood, an employer will not be entitled to its fees if it prevails.

TAXES

In almost all circumstances, a judicial monetary award or a settlement payment under the ADEA will be considered to be wages and, thus, will be subject to state and federal income taxes. Accordingly, an employer is obligated to withhold payroll and income taxes from such awards or payments. Before making a payment to an ADEA claimant, an employer should consult its counsel or tax adviser.

STATE LAW CLAIMS

In many cases, a former employee will attempt to bring a state law claim for age discrimination, or some other state law claim, based on the same facts as his or her ADEA claim. This claim usually is made in an attempt to obtain unlimited emotional distress and punitive damages. Although these types of claims often can be defeated before reaching trial, employers should be aware of the possibility for large verdicts resulting from related state law claims.